John Segal

You are holding in your hands a treasure. John Segal, with unrelenting practicality, shows a path forward for young people not to survive in this world but to thrive. His words of wisdom extend far past the weekly paycheck of annual salary. This book is a game plan for wise, meaningful living. The young people in your life should read it—and practice it.

—Ronnie McBrayer
Author, pastor, and nationally syndicated columnist

POOR
SMART
RICH

Moving *from* Poverty *to* Middle Class *and* Beyond

John M. Segal

Published by
Tremendous Leadership
in partnership with Gull House Press LLC

Gull House Press

Published by Tremendous Leadership
P.O. Box 267, Boiling Springs, PA 17007
www.TremendousLeadership.com
717-701-8159

This publication is designed to provide competent and reliable information regarding the subject matter covered. However, it is sold with the understanding that neither the author nor the publisher are engaged in rendering legal, financial, psychological, or other professional advice. Laws and practices often vary from state to state and if legal, financial, or other expert assistance is required, the services of a professional should be sought. The author and publisher specifically disclaim any liability that is incurred from the use or application of the contents of this book.

Library of Congress Cataloging-in-Publication Data

Name: Segal, John M.
Title: *POOR.SMART.RICH*
Library of Congress Control Number: 2017959234
Paperback ISBN: 978-1-936354-58-0
Ebook ISBN: 978-1-936354-61-0

All Bible quotations are from the King James Version.

To my wife, Sara,

and to my sons, Jason and Michael

Contents

PREFACE

My life did not start out well. I was not a good student, a gifted athlete, or a natural leader; our family was not well off. My parents were not around much during my childhood; they both worked multiple jobs.

We did not live in nice neighborhoods; I remember being scared much of the time when I was growing up. Like many others who grow up under similar circumstances, I thought I was destined to live like this for the rest of my life.

WHAT THIS BOOK IS ABOUT

> THIS BOOK IS ABOUT YOU—
> HOW YOU CAN FIND SUCCESS AND GET THE THINGS YOU
> WANT IN LIFE, EVEN IF IT SEEMS IMPOSSIBLE RIGHT NOW.
> I WAS ABLE TO CHANGE MY LIFE FOR THE BETTER—
> AND SO CAN YOU!

In this book, you will learn how to get out and stay out of poverty. You will learn how to move into the middle class and beyond. You will learn what it means to live a rich and abundant life and how to handle your money once you reach that life. You will learn that poor people and rich people do most of the same things in life, but the rich have learned to do them in a particular sequence—a special order—which gives them a great advantage.

1

This book is written for young people, from middle school through young adulthood. Many young Americans just like you started with nothing and got to a better life. My own business career was not flashy or spectacular, but it got me to that better life. There is nothing in this book that requires special talent. Any average young American can achieve everything I talk about in this book, and many already have.

The original idea for *POOR.SMART.RICH* came from lessons I learned teaching Sunday school classes to middle school and high school students over a nineteen-year period. This book also includes insights I gained working with, and speaking for, the National Fatherhood Initiative for eighteen years and from thirty-five years of owning and running a business with my brother.

Each year I asked my Sunday school students what they wanted to learn. They said they wanted to know practical things about real life—how to earn a good living, get the right education, get a good job, find a great person to marry, have a loving family, and deal with fear and frustration. They wanted to know how to reach a rich and abundant life. They did not want to be *told* what to do, but they were very interested in learning about the *consequences* of their choices and actions in life.

THE MINIMUM GOALS

The classes were built around six simple and powerful rules that are basic to good living. The first three rules are *minimum goals*—rules that will get you out and keep you out of poverty:

1. **PREGNANCY:** Don't get pregnant or get someone pregnant before high school graduation and marriage.
2. **WORK:** Get a job (almost any job) and build on it.
3. **MARRIAGE:** Get married and stay married.

These three rules are covered first because if you do not know and follow these rules FIRST, from an early age, you will greatly damage your chances of ever reaching a rich and abundant life.

Merely staying out of poverty, however, will not get you the kind of life you want. Many people work hard all their lives, staying just above the poverty line, and still end up broke and disappointed. To move beyond this

2

middle ground of survival, you must move to the higher ground of security and achievement—the *higher goals*.

THE HIGHER GOALS

The *higher goals* are the rules that allow young people to make the leap into the middle class and beyond to secure a rich and abundant life:

1. **WORK SMART:** Work hard on your job, but work harder on improving yourself.
2. **SET GOALS:** Write down your life goals and concentrate on achieving them.
3. **SEEK GOD:** Seek a positive, powerful relationship with God.

These rules are simple, but they are not easy.

That's why I wrote this book—to explain how you can use these six basic rules to live a better life, and how many others already have. There is nothing "experimental" about these rules of life; I have used them myself to achieve a better life. They are tested and true.

A WORD OF CAUTION

For those who dream of making it out of poverty and into financial security by becoming a celebrity or pro athlete, I don't know if this book will help. If you do have those rare abilities, I wish you the best of luck, but you need to know that your chances of making it in those kinds of careers are *very low*.

Odds of becoming:
NFL player (9 in 10,000), NBA player (3 in 10,000),
major league baseball player (1 in 6,600),
rock star (1 in 10,000), movie star (1 in 1,190,000).

The vast majority of successful people escape poverty and reach abundance by becoming teachers, plumbers, lawyers, airplane pilots, electricians, doctors, construction workers, computer technicians, nurses, and small business owners. Your chances of making it in these kinds of jobs are very good, because the world has a much greater need for these kinds of skills. Your knowledge and experience in these careers can lead to an ever-increasing income throughout your life.

Making money is an important part of a rich and abundant life because it gives you more choices, but money is only part of the solution. Along with the tools and insights to help you get ahead financially, this book will also teach you truths that will help you get more fun out of life. You were never meant for a life of drudgery, poverty, and failure, but of excitement and success.

This book is all about YOUR life:
what YOU want to do and who YOU want to be.
Believe me, YOU CAN DO THIS.

PART I: PAST AND PRESENT

RUNNING IN THE WRONG DIRECTION

We always called it the "alley-house"—an old two-story house sided with brown asphalt shingles, sitting on an unpainted, cinder-block basement in Milwaukee, Wisconsin, the town where I was born.

The owner lived in the house in front—the one on the street. Our family rented the one in the back—on the alley. The old house was heated by a coal furnace in the basement. In the winter, my dad had to shovel coal into the furnace every morning and every night to keep the heat going so we wouldn't freeze.

The second floor of the alley-house was an unfinished attic where my brother, Steve, and I slept at night. There were no heating ducts on that floor, so ice would form on the walls every winter. Mom would turn on the gas oven before she got us up in the morning, and Steve and I would run downstairs to stand in front of the open oven door to warm ourselves while we dressed. We took our baths in a galvanized washtub in the basement.

My brother tells the story about a man from the electric company showing up to turn off the power because we hadn't made the payment, and of Mom crying and pleading with him as he did it. Since I was only four, I don't remember that.

Mom and Dad both worked full-time jobs. Dad was struggling to start a small manufacturing business, and Mom worked as a secretary. I went to a Catholic kindergarten, and my older brother went to the public grade school. We weren't Catholic, but a group of Austrian nuns offered an inexpensive day-care near the building where Mom worked. I learned to sing Christmas carols with an Austrian accent. The nuns were nice and they fed us well. Mom always arrived late to pick me up after she left work, and the nuns constantly complained to her about her tardiness.

By the time my mother and I got home, my brother had already been there, alone, for hours. He was the original latchkey kid. His school let out much earlier than mine, so he would walk home, turn on the radio (we didn't have a TV), and hide under my parents' bed when it got dark. It got better for him when I was old enough to go to the first grade because we could walk home from school and wait at home together until Mom and Dad got home from work.

Since Mom worked all year long, she hired a babysitter to watch after my brother and me during the summer. The babysitter locked us out of the house all day so she could listen to "rock-n-roll" on the radio with her girlfriend. We never told Mom about the sitter because this allowed us to roam free with no adult control. We would walk the MRT (Milwaukee Rapid Transit) tracks, because it was the direct route to everywhere fun. The MRT was an elevated commuter rail system, which traveled at 50–60 miles an hour between stops. The tracks over the four-lane highways were only ties and rails. There were no walkways. If you were in the middle of the overpass when you heard the train whistle, you were in trouble.

My brother and the other kids could run on the open ties because they were bigger, but I was only five or six so I had to jump from one tie to the next. Steve tells of watching me from the end of the overpass one day as I hopped the ties with a screaming MRT throwing sparks and smoke from its locked wheels as the conductor desperately tried to stop. My brother grabbed me and pulled me off the tracks as I reached the end of the overpass. I didn't understand why he was crying. I felt the wind of the cars as they whipped by, but I wasn't scared. Helpless, he could see the train coming—I was concentrating on the ties and only heard it.

They actually backed the train up that day because the conductor thought he had hit me. We ran, of course, before the cops got there. The incident was reported in the *Milwaukee Journal*, with grave warnings to parents. Mom read it aloud to Steve and me. "No, Mom, we would never do anything like that. Honest. We were just playing in the yard." There is a scene in the movie *Stand By Me* where a similar incident is acted out by older boys. That movie, written by Stephen King, is a pretty accurate description of what life was like when I was growing up.

We would sneak under the fence of the Wisconsin State fairground and make friends with the "carny people." Early in the morning before the fairgrounds opened, the rollercoaster mechanic would let us ride the coaster he was "testing" at no charge. He would run it around five or six times without stopping—I usually threw up by then.

We hiked miles on the MRT, brought home railroad spikes, stray dogs, road signs, and great stuff we found in the "alley bins" which we always scanned for treasure prior to trash pickup. Our best finds were unused railroad flares and lanterns left at trackside by the caboose men. The flares looked like sticks of dynamite and would ignite in brilliant red sparking flames. We found a whole crate of flares one day, carried them home, and hid them under our beds. They had a spike at the bottom and an igniter at the top—once lit, they would burn through almost anything—even under water.

We crawled into grain elevators, ice-block houses, rail cars, warehouses, and onto any rooftop that was accessible. When adults discovered us, they would yell and start to chase us, but we were way too fast and knew escape routes they never dreamed existed.

When I was eight we moved to Illinois, and the town we lived in was about thirty minutes from St. Louis. For the first three months, we lived with my grandparents until we could find a place of our own. The town was a rough industrial area to grow up in. When my parents would drive into the city, I remember seeing the huge "shantytown" under the bridges in East St. Louis—wood crates, cardboard, and tin shacks that went on for miles. Thousands of people lived down there. It was like slums in third world countries today.

In Illinois, my dad had to start his business all over again. He worked fourteen to sixteen hours every day, including Saturdays and most Sundays. We saw him mainly on major holidays. Mom worked all day, too, but was usually home by 5:30 or 6:00 and on Sundays. My brother and I pretty much grew up on our own, and had no idea that this was unusual.

As kids, we got into a lot of trouble. I remember being afraid that the cops would show up at our house one day, because of some of the stuff we were doing. The kids we hung out with always had cigarettes they had taken from home, and occasionally one of the group showed up with a bottle of wine or beer, which got passed around.

We stole poker chips from the dime store and took them up on the second floor roof downtown, across the street from the Edwardsville Café. The cafe had a double door, and our challenge was to wing a poker chip from the roof across the street just as someone was opening the doors so that the chip would sail all the way into the cafe. It was a tough throw, and you had to get just the right spin on release. When we would succeed, people would come outside to try and figure out where the poker chips were coming from. Never thinking to look up at the roof across the street, they seemed to accept it as a strange periodic weather condition. Peeking over the edge of the roof across the street, we would collapse into laughter until our sides hurt. One day we got three chips into the cafe at once. What luck—a perfect trifecta!

We never really talked about it, but I guess we were poor. We weren't shantytown poor, but as we were growing up my brother and I began to realize that many families had better homes and cars than we did. This became more apparent as we got older. We were the last of all of our friends to get a television. We didn't lack for food, and we always had a place to live, but the food and clothes were simple, much like our homes and cars.

Although there wasn't much parental supervision at our house, we didn't feel abandoned or unloved. We knew our parents were working hard to make things better for us, not because they told us, but because we could see it year after year. We lived in rough neighborhoods, and the street-hardened kids who lived all around us were not a good influence. Most of those kids did not break out from that environment. If I had stayed with those kids and my life had continued on that early path, it would not have turned out well. I thank God that this did not happen.

When I was twelve we moved to Indiana. We lived in a rented sixty-foot trailer in the Evergreen Trailer Park. Where the name "Evergreen" came from is beyond me; there was not a green tree or bush in the whole place, just an acre of gravel, dirt, rock, and trailers. After about a year of scrimping and saving, my parents bought a small four-room house. Though it had only one bathroom and a detached garage, it felt like a castle after living in the trailer.

In Indiana my life slowly began to improve. Until that time I had been running in the wrong direction. When you grow up in rough neighborhoods without much supervision from parents, it's easy to develop bad ideas and get into trouble by following the crowd.

The town we moved to in Indiana was not a rough neighborhood; it had good schools, low crime, high employment, and honest, hardworking people with strong commitments to faith. At first I didn't fit in, but gradually I was able to change, which led to great improvements in my life. In this book, I will share some of the important stories about how this change took place.

Being poor is different now than when I grew up. There aren't nearly as many people actually living in poverty as there were then. The shantytowns under the bridges in East St. Louis are gone.

Today there are many welfare programs intended to help the poor. Though such programs have dramatically decreased the number of people living in poverty, they have created real barriers to moving from poor to middle class and beyond. Many people are now trapped in a low-level lifestyle, dependent on government support, and they don't know how to break out of it.

While the conditions of poverty may have changed, I don't believe the ways of getting out and staying out of poverty have changed. Getting out and staying out of poverty is absolutely necessary to reaching the good life you want and need. Getting trapped in poverty often happens through bad personal choices at a young age, so first we will focus on how to stay out of poverty.

HOW POVERTY WORKS

I f you want to have a really good life, your first step is to make sure you stay out of poverty. To stay out of poverty, you need to understand what it is and how it works.

HOW IS POVERTY DEFINED IN AMERICA?

Our government considers a US household to be in poverty if the annual income is LESS THAN the following:

- One person living alone: $12,060
- Family of three people: $20,420
- Family of four people: $24,600[1]

These figures are government estimates of the minimum income it takes to *survive* in our country. The first part of this book, then, is not about how to live a *great* life, but how to avoid living a really *lousy* life. (How to live a great and abundant life is discussed in Part II.)

If you're poor, welfare probably seems like a good idea—a monthly supplement to your income. And if your income is low enough to qualify, you can also receive food stamps (SNAP), free or subsidized housing, medical benefits (Medicaid) and more. If the government is willing to give it to you, why not take it?

Like a lot of things that are supposedly "free," there's a "catch" to taking welfare. To understand this, you have to know how the welfare system really works. In America, getting public assistance is no longer just a matter of being poor; it requires that you become part of the welfare system.

AVOIDING THE WELFARE TRAP

The American welfare system is complicated—very complicated. It changes depending on which state you live in, the number of people in your family, the ages of your children, and many other things. In addition to the federal regulations, every state has its own set of complicated rules.

It is impossible to give an example that applies to everyone, but the following are some general examples. Stick with me through this, and you will understand why I call it a "trap."

Let's imagine you have a part-time job working twenty hours a week. You get paid $6.25 per hour and you work in the mornings, so you have afternoons off to do what you want. This means you will earn $500 a month ($6,000 per year). But the local welfare office tells you it will *give* you an extra $500 a month so you don't have to live in poverty, and you will still have every afternoon off.

This means welfare has *doubled* your income to $12,000 a year, and you still only work twenty hours a week (1040 hours per year), so your income per hour worked has now doubled to $12.50 an hour. What a deal!

> $12,000 per year divided by 1040 hours
> per year = $12.50 per hour worked

Now let's say a full-time job opens up, and your boss offers it to you, adding that there could be opportunities for advancement. Your hourly rate stays the same ($6.25), but now you are working forty hours a week—no afternoons off. The amount you earn from working more hours goes to $1000 per month ($12,000 per year). But now that you are earning more money, the welfare office cuts the amount they give you from $500 a month to $200 a month. This means that you will get $12,000 a year from working but only $2,400 a year from welfare (put together, you will be getting $14,400 per year).

$$\$14,400 \text{ per year divided by } 2080 \text{ hours}$$
$$\text{per year} = \$6.92 \text{ per hour worked}$$

What is the net result? You have earned a little more income for a lot more work. You gained $500 a month by doubling your work hours, but you lost $300 a month that welfare was giving you for NO work. You just gave up your afternoons off for sixty-seven cents an hour![2]

This is how welfare works. The work, though it will give you more experience and make you more valuable to employers in the future, actually causes you to lose welfare benefits. Not only will you lose welfare, which isn't taxed, but your taxes increase on the money you earn from working. If you rely on other government assistance programs (food stamps, Medicaid, etc.), these benefits may be reduced or eliminated as well because of your higher earned income, and the situation only becomes worse.

Let's look at a more common example. Imagine you are a single parent with two small children, both under age five. You didn't graduate from high school, and you don't have a job. You go to the local welfare office and ask for help. They sign you up for all the welfare you are qualified to receive—after all, that is their job. The value of the welfare package they give you is $28,500 a year.[3] This is the same as earning $12.50[4] per hour at a full-time job, but you won't have to actually work to get this welfare in most cases.[5]

If getting into the welfare system gives you enough money and other benefits to get you "out of poverty," why not just kick back, take the government's money, and forget about working? Here is the reason:

TO STAY ON WELFARE, YOU HAVE TO STAY POOR.

Welfare is a trap because the programs are "means-tested." As you get more of your own "means" (earned income and savings), you lose big chunks of welfare. If you really start working and getting ahead, you lose all your benefits. Any success in life feels like you are just running in place. The harder you work, the more benefits welfare takes away.

15

But wait, it gets worse. Imagine you are that single parent with two little children on welfare. You meet someone who has a job with a good income, and you'd like to get married. They had better have a *very* good income, because you will probably lose all or most of your welfare. Remember, welfare is "means tested"—if you marry the person, their income ("means") will be added to yours, which will probably push you over the income limit, and you won't qualify for welfare anymore. It's called the "welfare marriage penalty."

Suddenly your family of three on welfare becomes a family of four (or more) without welfare, perhaps with only a little more income than you used to get on welfare. What will the person you want to marry say when they find out that they have to make up for the $28,500 a year you will lose if you get married?

This has become a major incentive to avoid marriage and settle for a live-in partner—a common and growing situation. Not getting married to the person you love and just living together is a terrible decision for you and your children. It leaves families without security, exposing children to poverty, confusion, and fear. Unmarried couples living together more often lack the commitment needed to create lasting and secure families in which children prosper.[6]

All the incentives in the welfare system are backward, structured to keep you *in* poverty, instead of helping you get *out*. It's not because our government hates poor people; it's because the welfare system is a patchwork of unconnected programs, put together over many years, and lacking any well designed plan to help people develop the knowledge and skills needed to escape poverty. (For more about how welfare programs work in America, see Appendix E.)

The lesson is pretty clear: you can't count on the government to get you out of poverty with welfare programs. There are ways you can stay out of poverty, however, which we will cover a little later in this book.

You need to know these things because the welfare trap can catch you at a very young age. Most young people who fall into this trap don't even know it exists until they make a few bad decisions and find themselves caught. Like you, they had dreams of a better life—of getting an education,

16

having a family, and living in a safe neighborhood. They had dreams of providing a better life for their children than they had. They didn't end up on welfare because they were lazy and unwilling to work to reach their dreams. In most cases, welfare started out as a temporary answer to a bad situation, and seemed like the only choice. But you can avoid this trap if you understand how it happens.

How do so many young people fall into the welfare trap every year? Why do they fail to see the consequences of their own choices? The story of Shiana and Marik may help you understand how this can happen.[7]

SHIANA: I was sixteen when I got pregnant the first time. I mean it's like I know it's best to wait 'til after high school to have kids, and get married and everything. But it just sort of happened—the baby, I mean. I was really happy I was pregnant, but I was scared too.

It was really great at first. Me and Marik done everything together. It was perfect. We were pretty wild I guess—skippin' school, rippin' and runnin' around, partying and drinking and drugs. But that changed when the baby came. The baby made me settle down, grow up.

Yes, we used contraception real careful at first—both of us— but he didn't like the condoms. We weren't as careful after a while, after we were exclusive, just dating each other and nobody else. The baby was sort of an accident, unplanned—and sort of not. I mean like we talked about it and everything. He said if anything went wrong, don't worry, he'd take care of it—you know, pay for everything, take care of us, be like a family. I always wanted to have babies and be a real family.

MARIK: She used to be great, really wild, a blast. We were good together—did everything together. We had a lot of great times. But the baby, that was her. She told me she was using pills, contraception, and I used my stuff at first too, real careful. How can you get pregnant when you're taking the pill all the time? I mean we talked about it. I told her if anything happened don't worry, I'd pay for it—you know, the abortion. We both knew we didn't want kids yet.

SHIANA: My parents were really, really mad at me not waiting. Mom talked all the time about waiting for kids, finishing school first.

My dad's not my real dad. But then Mom helped out a lot. Marik got real mad when I told him about the baby—I mean shouting and breaking stuff and everything. That jerk stopped coming around most of the time when I was pregnant. I heard he was dating my best friend, but he says he didn't. Then he shows up at the hospital when the baby was born, all excited, and said he wanted to get back together again, so I did. I mean I had the baby and everything. But then he was always angry and drinking a lot more. Marik could get kind of violent like that. You couldn't say nothing to him. He said it was my fault he had to quit going to college and get a job. But he never got a good job. He wasn't working enough hours.

MARIK: When the baby came Shiana really changed. We were living in her mom's apartment. She wouldn't ever go out and party anymore—just wanted to stay at home with the baby. She went nuts every time I wanted to go out with my friends. I mean, like, I got a job and I'd buy stuff for the baby and everything, but it's never enough for her. She always wants more and better; so what's the use? I wanted to go back to school—I was doing OK—but then I couldn't save anything up for that.

SHIANA: Having the baby made me grow up, be responsible. I can't be drinkin' and druggin'. I'm going to be there for my baby. I don't get why he didn't settle down. I mean, like, it's his kid too. He needs to get more work—and better work—grow up. Welfare's not enough. Babies don't live on just love—it takes money.

MARIK: I really wanted to get back together when I saw the baby, and we did, for a while. But she totally changed with the baby. I finally got fed up. I couldn't do anything right for her. It was never enough. Yeah, I found somebody better to date. Shiana called the Child Support on me at work—you can't talk with her, she never listens. It's always about her—what she wants, what she needs. I need stuff too.

SHIANA: He stuck around for a few months after the baby came, but he was different—always angry. He wasn't providing anything good—just used stuff, used clothes, used crib. I can get welfare for that much and don't have to put up with him. I'm proud that I never married that idiot. I met a new guy, and he has a good job. I'm pregnant again, but he's sticking with it. He cares about the baby, and it isn't even his. We ain't getting married and lose the benefits. I'm going to take some classes and get a GED when this kid is born. I always wanted to be a nurse some day; maybe get married, when we can do it right—have a big wedding. I love my baby. I'm there for her. Life's pretty screwed up right now, but you just have to go with it. Nothing else you can do. At least I have my baby—something of my own.

Unfortunately, Shiana and Marik's story is not that unusual. They didn't intend to fall into a life of poverty and dependence on other people; they just didn't have a plan. They talked about contraception, and about what would happen if there was a "problem" (pregnancy), but did they really agree on that? Can you begin to see how the lack of agreement on a good plan for their lives trapped Shiana and Marik in poverty?

I can predict the rest of Shiana and Marik's story based on what happens to most people in this situation. Shiana will "be there for her children," just as she has promised, struggling to provide them with clean clothes, food, and a place to live (with Shiana's mom). Shiana will hold her family together while they are toddlers, but once the children start school, they will begin to slip away from Shiana's control and influence.

Her children will go to poor schools in rough neighborhoods; they will need to get tough to deal with the bad influences around them. She will try to warn them not to get pregnant, to stay away from drugs, and to finish school. She will even use herself as a bad example. But they will not listen to her, because kids pay more attention to what parents do than what they say.

Shiana will get her GED, and after the kids are grown, she will even get a two-year degree in nursing. The nursing degree will allow her to get a decent job for the first time in her life. Had she landed this job before her children were born, she could have afforded to move to a good neighborhood where her children would have had better schools and more opportunity. But it is too late now. She will have to use her new job to support herself, her unmarried daughter and two grandchildren, who live with her. Her job will also pay for a lawyer to defend her son on drug charges. Later in life she will eventually get married, but not to the father of her children.

As for Marik, he will drift in and out of Shiana's life, providing most, but not all, of the court-ordered child support. Marik will finish two years of college and get a semi-skilled job. He will also get married later in life and have more children. Like Shiana, he will be poor all his life.

Shiana and Marik will do all the things in life that successful, middle-class people do—but in a way which will always keep them poor. They will do them in the wrong order, in a way that creates, rather than solves, problems.

This does not need to be your story. There is a better way.

PART II: POOR

AVOIDING THE TRAP

HOW TO STAY OUT OF POVERTY: MINIMUM GOALS

Following *three simple rules* will greatly increase the chances for you and your family to get out and stay out of poverty. As you read the three rules remember that I said they were simple; I didn't say they were easy. I will tell you what the rules are, but they are not my rules. I'm already out of poverty. If you want to stay out of poverty, you have to make these *your* rules. And, you have to be tough enough and smart enough to resist those who try to get you to break your rules.

Who will try to get you to break your rules? Many people, for their own selfish reasons. Some will try to get you to break your rules because they themselves have not been able to keep them. If you can keep them and they can't, you will be showing them up by being stronger, smarter, and more capable than they are. Don't let them get away with that! Real friends—good friends—would never treat you that way.

The welfare system is also a very powerful encouragement to break these rules. Welfare may look like an easy way out, but it can be a trap that is hard to escape. You need to be strong enough and smart enough to avoid that trap. Following these three rules is the best way to do that.

No one expects much of young people these days. What a mistake! From teaching teens, I have discovered that they are capable of more than adults expect of them, and FAR more than they expect of themselves. If you use your teen years as I describe in this book, you can set yourself up for a life of excitement and success. Stop fooling yourself. You are stronger and more capable than you think—YOU CAN DO THIS.

RULE ONE: PREGNANCY

Don't get pregnant or get someone pregnant before high school graduation and marriage

When Congress passed the "War on Poverty" legislation in September 1964, about 19 percent of Americans were poor.[8] The theory was that by spending money to help poor people, we could end poverty in our country. But in 2014, fifty years after these laws were passed, the poverty rate in America was only down to 14.3 percent.[9] It is estimated that our government has now spent about $19 trillion dollars on the "War on Poverty."*

After spending all of this money to help poor Americans, why are there still so many families living in poverty? A major reason for this is that there has been a dramatic increase in the number of young unmarried women raising small children. U.S. Bureau of Census figures show that *being raised in a married family reduces a child's probability of living in poverty by 80 percent*.[10]

When the War on Poverty started, most young women were married when they became pregnant, or got married soon after.[11] In the 1960s, the number of unmarried women having children began to increase rapidly.[12] There are many reasons for this change, including increased casualness about sex due to birth control and legal abortions. New anti-poverty programs also began paying money to support single mothers, but often took that money away if the mother got married.[13]

*See Appendix E for more information on the welfare system in America.

The reasons behind this explosion of young, unmarried moms doesn't really make any difference *for you*. Only the *results* make a difference *for you*. And the results of getting pregnant or getting your girlfriend pregnant and staying unmarried will have terrible and long-lasting effects on your life, and on the life of your children.

Don't try to say you "didn't mean to get pregnant," or "it just happened," or "I couldn't help myself." Nonsense! It happens because you either want to it to happen or you don't care enough about your own life to *make a decision and stick to it*.[14]

> YOU DO NOT GET PREGNANT OR GET
> SOMEONE PREGNANT WITHOUT MAKING
> A DECISION TO HAVE SEX

Deciding to have sex is not something you leave to a "moment of passion." It is a decision you make before then.* You make the decision and then avoid getting into a situation you can't handle.

If you don't trust yourself to do this, or you are too weak-willed to make and keep this decision with yourself, there are many cheap and available means[15] to prevent MOST pregnancies, but none of them are safe and effective 100 percent of the time.[16] And if you do choose to take this more dangerous route, contraception is not something you leave to your partner—it is *your* responsibility and *yours alone*—every time. *Never* trust contraception to the other person.

THINK—what do you want your life to be like? Most people want the same good things out of life. They want to:

- FIRST: ***Get an education*** (high school diploma, minimum).
- SECOND: ***Have a decent job,***
- THIRD: ***Find a good partner to marry,***
- FOURTH: ***Have children,*** and

---

* **Note:** pregnancy caused by rape, which occurs in about 5 percent of rapes, is a separate issue, which we are not dealing with in this book. Pregnancy from rape is caused by a criminal assault and is not the fault of the victim.

- FIFTH: Live in a **_safe neighborhood_** with **_good schools._**

However, the key to getting these things without falling into poverty is the order in which they are done. Shiana and Marik did most of these things, but in the wrong order.

```
┌─────────────────────────────────────────────┐
│                                               │
│         PEOPLE WHO SUCCEED IN LIFE            │
│         DO THINGS IN A SPECIAL ORDER.         │
│                                               │
└─────────────────────────────────────────────┘
```

What is this special order?[17] It is the five steps underlined above. Most Americans do most of these things at some time in their life.[18] But if you try to do them in the wrong order, your chances of a rich and abundant life will be very low. And the worst one of these things to get out of order is having children first.

Having a baby can be one of the most fulfilling things in life, but only if you are prepared to take good care of that baby. Some people think that having a baby first will bring them the love, companionship, and structure they want and need in their lives. But having a baby *first* hampers your ability to reach the other good things in life—and it makes life harder for your child. This kind of thinking is disastrous; *it is completely backward, and it is responsible for most of the poverty in America.*

Having a baby when you are poor makes you poorer. Bringing a baby into a home without enough money, adequate food, and decent housing will never solve your problems—it will only increase them. Life becomes harder when you are young, unmarried, and have a small child to care for. Small children take up your time and money. It's much more difficult, perhaps even impossible, to finish high school (or college). Keeping a job is more difficult, because you have less free time and added costs for child care. Having a baby makes you more dependent on other people for help, because your time and money have to be spent on the baby.

What about the father's "shared responsibility"? Sorry, ladies—in most cases, the father disappears. Even if you can locate him, it will be a fight to get him to pay the court-ordered child support. *Less than 20 percent of fathers who aren't married at the time of the child's birth will even be around five years after the child is born.*[19]

WEAK LIFE PLAN

ATTITUDE
Things Just Happen
Go with the Flow
I Want Children / Marriage Can Wait

CHANCES OF SUCCESS:
20% or less

1	♡	Girl Meets Boy
2	**SEX**	Not Carefully Protected WEAK AGREEMENT
3	👶	Pregnancy and Birth Girl Drops out of School
4	WELFARE	Girl Gets on Welfare
5	💔	Partner Leaves Girl Lives with Relatives
6	♡	Girl Meets New Guy
7	💔👶	No Marriage So Girl Can Keep Welfare
8	👶💔	More Guys, More Kids, More Welfare
9	💉🔫	Live in Rough Neighborhood Bad Schools/High Crime

MOST LIKELY RESULT:
Disorder, Welfare, Poverty
Poor Children with Problems

POVERTY

STRONG LIFE PLAN

ATTITUDE
I Can Plan a Good Life
I Am Strong/ I Can Make It Happen
I Want Children but Only After Marriage

CHANCES OF SUCCESS:
80% or more

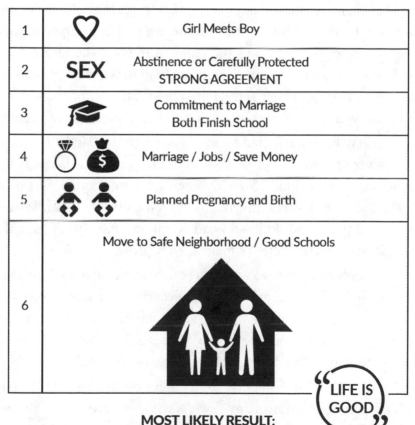

1	♡	Girl Meets Boy
2	SEX	Abstinence or Carefully Protected STRONG AGREEMENT
3		Commitment to Marriage Both Finish School
4		Marriage / Jobs / Save Money
5		Planned Pregnancy and Birth
6		Move to Safe Neighborhood / Good Schools

"LIFE IS GOOD"

MOST LIKELY RESULT:
Marriage, Family, Abundance
Secure Children with Opportunities

Unmarried fathers have very few legal *rights* to their children, but they sure have legal *responsibilities*. Failing to pay child support can get your wages garnished (withheld), your passport denied, liens placed on your home, your driver's license revoked, your vehicle seized, your credit rating ruined, and get you criminally prosecuted.[20]

Child support lasts for at least eighteen years—and much longer if the child is born with health problems or special needs. It's a life spent sitting in Family Court, paying lawyers, and listening to judges tell you how you are going to live.

There is no reason for any young man to get himself stuck with this kind of a burden. You can be the one who takes charge of your life choices. Your character and strength can provide the leadership your girlfriend wants and expects so you can both make the right choices for your life. Taking charge and taking responsibility for these decisions will grow you into the person you have always dreamed of becoming.

You may have never had a dad around to protect and encourage you as you were growing up, but you can be the one who keeps that from happening to your kids. Your children will need a dad, just as much as you did, and that is a gift that only you can give them. You don't have to be perfect to do it—no dad is; all you have to do is make the commitment and be there for them as they grow.

You don't have to have a life stuck in welfare poverty. You can have the marriage, children, and financial security you want—but it won't happen by chance. You have to do some thinking and planning. There is a very clear difference in the way successful people go about getting what they want. The Life Choice Charts on pages 28—29 show the difference—they show the *special order* for staying out of poverty.

Pay attention to how many fewer steps there are on the Strong Life Plan side. Life is so much easier when you understand the "special order" of doing things. Choose a strong life plan, and make the decision to stay out of poverty.

You can see that the biggest difference between the two Life Choice Charts starts with your *attitude*, especially when it comes to marriage and children. If your attitude reflects the Weak Life Plan, you need to change it *right now!* Adjusting your attitude to the Strong Life Plan is the first and most important step you can take.

A Strong Life Plan increases your chances of getting out and staying out of poverty from less than 20 percent to more than 80 percent. That is about as close to a guarantee as you will ever get in life. These are FACTS:

> MARRIED COUPLES EXPERIENCE FAR LESS POVERTY IN AMERICA, REGARDLESS OF THEIR RACE, COLOR, OR CREED. [21]

Your attitude really comes into play with your decision about having children; you and your partner need to make a decision about sex. If you don't make a decision on this together, *you are choosing to stay on the weak side*. And deciding to stay on the weak side will most likely lead to welfare dependence and poverty.

You have to make this agreement together and talk about it often — it will make your relationship stronger and help you to know if this is the right person to have as a life partner. You don't need to be sexually "experienced" to have a strong marriage. In fact, studies show that having pre-marital sex with multiple partners actually decreases your chances of having a stable and lasting marriage.[22]

Talk about sex with your partner and make the right decision. Avoiding a pregnancy will give you the time to get to know each other and have a real relationship, one based on trust and understanding. It is the commitment to each other in marriage that makes it possible for you to have love, companionship, security, and structure in your life. It just doesn't work the other way around. Having a baby at a young age won't bring order to your life, and it won't make the relationship with your partner better—it will drive you apart.

31

WHAT WOULD YOUR CHILD SAY ABOUT YOUR WEAK LIFE PLAN?

Take a look at it from your child's point of view. If you chose a Weak Life Plan, he or she has only one parent to provide financial support, devoted guidance, and adult protection. In most cases women are the single parent left with the responsibility of raising the child, and the statistics for that child's health and safety are not good. Children growing up without fathers:

1. Are four times more likely to be poor when they grow up.[23]
2. Show higher levels of aggressive behavior.[24]
3. Have much higher odds of teenage delinquency[25] and adult time in prison.[26]
4. Have much higher teen rates of pregnancy.[27]
5. Experience many more incidents of child abuse (most often from live-in boyfriends).[28]
6. Have higher rates of obesity.[29]
7. Have higher rates of drug and alcohol abuse.[30]
8. Have lower school performance.[31]

Is this the kind of life you want for your child?

Most young, unmarried, pregnant women decide to drop out of school "temporarily," abandoning their original goals of higher education. This results in a lower ability to find a well-paying job. It traps a young woman and her children in rough, unsafe neighborhoods with poor schools and no opportunities.[32] It is physically and emotionally exhausting.

This doesn't mean that a single mother can't raise a child successfully, but it certainly is a lot harder without the help of an *involved, responsible*, and *committed* father. It is only logical that a single parent has less time, money, family support, and opportunity than two parents.

Shiana says that she's glad she "didn't marry that jerk Marik," but she wasn't so careful about having unprotected sex with him. Marik is the father of her daughter, so that "jerk" will be part of their lives forever. (You need to be careful about choosing the other parent of your children; improving your chances of doing this is discussed in the chapter on marriage.)

THINK ABOUT THIS: If you FIRST work at getting your education and a good job, it will make your other goals easier. It will be easier to find a caring companion who also has an education and a good income. Together, in a committed marriage, you will have the resources to make sure that your children can live in a safe community with good schools, where their friends will be a positive influence. If you make the right choices, there is no reason that you and your children will have to live in poverty in America. If you really want to love your child, go for the Strong Life Plan.

What if you have already violated this first rule—you're young, you have a baby and you're not married? Can you still stay out of poverty? Yes—but it will be more difficult.

RULE TWO: WORK

Get a job—almost any job—and build on it

I have a friend who owns and operates three fast-food restaurants for one of the big national chains. To operate one of his restaurant locations requires a staff of about 60 people. He could open more locations except for the fact that he can't hire enough employees. Many of his employees are part-time because they are students or have other jobs. My friend's biggest hiring problem is that he can't find enough good, reliable, *full-time* employees. The median hourly wage for people working in fast food restaurants is $9.15 per hour.[33] My friend actually offers other benefits such as medical coverage and paid vacations, but let's just use the $9.15 hourly wage as an example.

The annual income of a full-time employee at $9.15 per hour would be over $19,000. If two of these full-time employees get married, together they would make $38,000 per year. That is well above the poverty level.

Married Couple Working Full-Time Fast Food Jobs
She earns 9.15 per hour X 2080 hours =$19,000 per year
He earns 9.15 per hour X 2080 hours = <u>$19,000</u> per year
Together they earn $38,000 per year

Even if this married couple had two children, they would still be earning $13,400 (54 percent) *more* than the poverty level for a family of four. If you can live above the poverty level working in a fast food restaurant, why are so many people in poverty in America? There are several reasons.

THE WELFARE TRAP

One reason is that our government is competing for these workers with welfare. The worker might say, "Why shouldn't I just sit home and collect a welfare check instead of going to work every day for just a little more than I get on welfare?" That's a good question. The answer is simple, and it may be one of the most important things you ever learn about staying out of poverty:

> *You can get government handouts for doing nothing, but no one wants to hire a person who has no job experience and no ambition to improve.*

If you stay on welfare, you are stuck right where you are. You can't earn, or save, too much or the government will take away your welfare benefits. With welfare you really are stuck either in a low-paying job, or staying at home doing nothing *forever*. Welfare was supposed to be a way out of poverty, but it has become a poverty trap that will keep you down forever if you let it.

Am I saying that you should *not* use welfare if you are poor and need the help to survive? Not at all—use every honest means possible to survive and provide for your family. But also work, learn, and save as hard as you can to avoid welfare or to get off welfare as soon as possible. Welfare *is* poverty. The problem is that welfare *appears* to make work look like it gives you less financial return. But working and learning are the only ways you can get out and stay out of poverty.

> *Working part-time at a fast-food restaurant (or any other starter job) isn't a bed to lie down in; it's the first rung on the ladder to success.*

It is a place to start building your work history and your skills. To a future employer, it shows that you can get to work on time every day and work effectively with other people. If you decide to stay in the fast-food business, and your work performance is better than others, you might even be able to move to a manager position. In a management position, you will get training and experience supervising other people, and you can rise in the management of your franchise group. You may be smart enough and become skilled enough in the fast-food business to own your own franchised restaurant in the future.

Do you think I'm exaggerating your possibilities for success? Let me tell you about another friend of mine who is also in the fast-food business. During high school, Bob worked at a grocery store. After graduation, he continued working at the grocery and later took a job as the meat cutter at a local IGA. Bob and a fellow employee signed up for a Dale Carnegie course, and after one of the evening classes they went out to see if they could find a good hamburger. They couldn't find one and started to think this might be a business opportunity. They decided to become partners and open a fast-food restaurant of their own.

Business at their restaurant gradually increased and it became profitable. Bob worked hard, and discovered that he really liked the restaurant business. He and his partner started opening more fast-food restaurants, with Bob as the managing partner. Lovella, Bob's wife, did the accounting and bookkeeping, working in the basement of their home. After a few years, Bob's partner decided to sell his share of the restaurants to Bob. Working with his wife, Lovella, Bob promoted employees from within and built a growing team of managers for their expanding restaurant locations. Bob and Lovella now own 150 restaurants and employ more than 3,000 people. They continue to work hard and provide great careers and benefits to many young people.

With work experience, you have a chance to advance based on your ability. If you have job experience you can take advantage of new opportunities. You can never tell exactly when that opportunity will arrive or where it will come from, but it will never come if you are sitting home living on welfare. To continue receiving welfare, you have to stay poor and blame others for your lack of success.

THE UNEDUCATED

Another reason many people are in poverty is because they have made themselves unemployable by refusing to take school seriously and failing to learning the basics. They never learn to read, write, or do math well enough to keep a good job. In the past, there were manual labor jobs that paid a decent wage and didn't require basic reading and writing skills, but that's just not the case anymore.

In April 2014, the U.S. Department of Education and the National Institute of Literacy completed a study of reading skills. They found that thirty-two million Americans—14 percent of the population— can't read.[34] Does that figure ring a bell? That's right—about the same percentage live in welfare poverty in America. That same study found that Americans with the lowest level of reading skills were only able to work half as many hours and received less than half the wage rate as those with better reading skills.[35] The connection is clear: if you can't read well, you won't do well in America. However, you can improve your reading skills at any age.

Basic education is available *for free* to every young person in America, *all the way through high school*. Dropping out of school is a huge mistake that will literally cost you a fortune.[36] Don't let "friends" tell you school doesn't matter. Don't let anyone bully you about making good grades in school. School is your last chance to get an education that is yours for the taking at no charge. Grab it, hold on to it, and find a way to make it work for you. You can do this!

You might think, "Well, I'm reading this book, so that is not my problem." But how *well* do you read? Did you know that 85 percent of defendants in the juvenile court system are functionally illiterate, and over 70 percent of inmates in American prisons cannot read above a fourth grade level?[37] They can read, but not well. Being able to read and understand *most* of the words is a start, but you have to get to at least a high school graduate reading level to make a decent living.

Almost all young people in America get an opportunity to learn these basic skills in school. But for various reasons, some fall behind and are too embarrassed to admit that they need help. You may have missed a lot of school because your family moved frequently, or you missed the basics and were just passed along (many high school *graduates* in America cannot read very well).[38] In many cases, people with these problems think they are dumb, because others around them have learned these things. Usually, however, they are smart enough; they have just not asked for the help they need and deserve. If this is your experience, I encourage you to find a way to get yourself basic education skills.

Are you satisfied with your ability to read, write and do basic math on at least a high school level? If not, and you are still in school, it is not too late to admit it and ask a teacher, a guidance counselor, or a friend for help. If you are out of school, there is help available (listed in Appendix A) to learn these basic skills—a necessity if you want to stay out of poverty. There is no way around this. You have to get an education to avoid the poverty trap—and you *can*.

ADDICTIONS

People also make themselves unemployable by abusing drugs and alcohol. The problem usually starts out small, and users think they can control it. But it tends to grow over time until it consumes larger and larger amounts of time and money. The reason for this is that small amounts of drugs give you a temporary good feeling—a "buzz"—but over time, it takes stronger and stronger doses, or sometimes even a stronger drug, to get the desired effect. (The same goes for alcohol, which is nothing more than a liquid drug, and can be just as addicting.)

As the addiction progresses, the drug becomes a growing part of your life, your central focus, and that is the real problem. When you lose your focus on the daily practices needed to maintain a good and stable life, your quality of life declines. This behavior destroys personal relationships; everyone but the abuser notices the change in personality.

No one will keep an employee who doesn't show up for work, or shows up drunk, drugged, or hung over. And other employees, the good ones, don't want to work around people like that. Drug convictions can stay on your record for decades and close the door to better jobs. An arrest for driving under the influence of drugs or alcohol (DUI) can cause you to lose your driver's license, cost you up to $10,000, go on your permanent police and driving record and make you ineligible for certain types of employment. That's a high price to pay for a "buzz."

In the Army, I worked in a drug rehab clinic for abusers returning from overseas deployment. The Army had an excellent program at that time, because there was a very great need: soldiers overseas could get all types of cheap drugs, and many developed addictions. I dealt with soldiers abusing alcohol, marijuana, LSD, heroin, and other drugs. Every one of them told me that they started out thinking they could just take a little of the drug and keep from getting hooked.

Some said their drug use was their own business and they weren't hurting anyone else. They thought they were exercising their free will—they couldn't see that the drugs were actually taking away their free will. They lost all control over the drugs; the drugs controlled them.

One sergeant told me that he used heroin in small amounts every now and then, and claimed he was not addicted. That's impossible. Heroin is one of the most addicting drugs out there. Most people are surprised to learn, however, that the physical addiction to heroin only lasts for two weeks after you quit. The physical addiction to any drug isn't the biggest problem. The mental craving and desire for the drug— psychological addiction—is much, much worse, and can last a lifetime.

Drug and alcohol addictions can destroy personal relationships and take years of costly treatment and counseling to overcome.[39] New and more powerful drugs like fentanyl (thirty to fifty times more powerful than heroin) and "spice" (synthetic marijuana) are constantly being developed, claiming new victims.[40] Many people die from addictions, but many more are stuck in long-lasting poverty, mental confusion, and depression. The best way to avoid this is to stay away from drugs *and* drug users. Life is hard enough; why add more problems to your life?

ATTITUDE

Another way you can make yourself unemployable is by always doing as little work as possible, sleeping on the job, or getting into arguments with other employees. These are things *you* can control, and it starts with your attitude. If you have a good attitude and try to do your best at work, it will be noticed. The truth is that in America, employers can't find enough good, reliable employees for all of the jobs that are available. And I am only talking about the bottom of the job market at this point. Think of the opportunities a little higher up in the job market for those who are ready and willing to put in the effort.

**DON'T TAKE A JOB ONLY FOR WHAT IT WILL PAY.
TAKE A JOB FOR WHAT IT WILL TEACH YOU.
WHAT YOU LEARN INCREASES YOUR VALUE
MORE THAN WHAT YOU EARN.**

My experience in the Army and in business tells me that the reason some people sleep on the job or just do as little as possible isn't because they are tired. I believe it is a form of rebellion, a way of saying, "I don't want to be here, so I'm going to do just enough to keep from getting fired." But a poor attitude like that is a good way to *get* fired.

A bad attitude is also the best way I can think of to make the workday drag out endlessly. When you are active, interested, and involved, time flies by. We have all experienced this. When you are watching the clock, at school or at work, the minutes seem like hours. So, if you really want your workday to *feel* shorter, get enthusiastic.

Make it a game. You can turn almost any work into a game by setting your own high standard for performance, and then trying to beat your own standards. Do this and I assure you that two things will happen: you will start to enjoy the work you are doing, and your improved performance will be noticed. Not only will your efforts be noticed by your manager, but also by other good employees. When this happens, don't be surprised if some of the not-so-good employees try to give you a hard time about it; but don't let yourself be bullied by the "not-so-goods" who are going nowhere.

Some people won't take a job they feel is "beneath" them. They consider it a put-down to start at the bottom, at low wages or doing manual labor. Since my first jobs were mopping floors, cleaning bathrooms, and painting machines, that attitude sounds ridiculous to me. Most of the successful people I know started out at low-level jobs, just as I did. If you wait for a job with "dignity," you will never get a starter job. Doing a low-level job well puts you on the road to high-level opportunities.

You don't get a job with dignity, you create
dignity in your job by doing it well.

DISABILITIES

What if you are disabled in some way—confined to a wheelchair, visually impaired, hearing impaired, dyslexic? What if you have attention deficit disorder, PTSD, speech problems, poor social skills, alcoholic parents, or some other issue? Sorry, it doesn't exempt you from life. Life goes on with or without you and your disabilities. It is up to you to figure out how to overcome these hardships. People do it every day and you can too!

Am I being too insensitive? Whether I am or not really doesn't change anything. You still have to deal with your own situation. My dad often shared this nugget of wisdom, whenever something bad happened to me or my brother:

> "YOU HAVE TO TAKE THINGS FROM WHERE THEY ARE,
> NOT FROM WHERE YOU WOULD LIKE THEM TO BE."

There was no arguing with that statement, but I can remember a few times when those words felt like a splash of cold water. What he was really saying was, "Wake up! Come back to reality! You can't change what happened, so deal with the problem, and stop wallowing in your anger, frustration, and resentment."

Life is not fair. It never has been, and it never will be. We are all born with different abilities and we all have different experiences throughout our lives. That's just the way it is. But if you take a look around, you will find many other people who faced far greater obstacles in life than you, and they still managed to succeed.

There is a young woman in my hometown named Kelly Craig Schaefer. She was a star athlete in high school, a nationally ranked cheerleader for Indiana University in college, and was studying to become a teacher. At the end of her sophomore year in college, she was on vacation with her family when a drunk driver smashed into their van. Kelly's injuries were life threatening; she survived, but was left a quadriplegic. She cannot get out of her wheelchair by herself; she cannot lift the book you are reading.

But that isn't the end of the story. Kelly went on to finish college and got a job teaching grade school. She also has a second career as a professional speaker, giving talks all around the country about the dangers of drinking and driving. More recently she got married, and she and her husband have adopted two children. If you think you have a disability that is holding you back, read her book, *Fractured Not Broken: A Memoir*.[41]

Most of the highly successful people I have met tell stories of having to overcome childhood poverty, physical disabilities, discrimination, abuse, learning problems, and every other kind of obstacle you can think of. Rather than letting those things hold them back, focusing on overcoming those obstacles seems to have been the driving force that moved them forward toward success. Their setbacks gave them a fighting spirit and a greater will to overcome their barriers.

I suspect that everyone has some form of "disability." When people really open up to you and tell you their life stories, it is amazing to hear the things they have overcome. If you can look beyond the surface to discover what is in a person's heart, I believe you will find that most are quite noble. More than a few people have told me of long, frustrating hours they have spent overcoming some type of difficulty that most of us have never had to face. If you look at obstacles as opportunities to build your skills, you'll gain an iron-clad confidence that you can achieve anything in life.

The foundation of success is attitude.

What if you have already violated the first and second rules? Can you still stay out of poverty? Yes, but it will be more difficult. Every rule you break adds an extra load you have to carry just to stay out of poverty. But you can do this.

RULE THREE: MARRIAGE

Get married and stay married

Why should I have to *get married* to stay out of poverty? Well, you don't *have to*. But remember, we are talking about *minimum* goals in this part of the book. It is simply a fact that your chances of living in poverty are much lower if you are married.[42] Why do you think this might be true?

One big reason is that being married gives you and your spouse the opportunity to earn two incomes. Remember our example of a guy working in a fast-food restaurant who marries a girl working in a fast-food restaurant? Together they earn twice as much as one person alone, but their expenses won't double when they get married. Together they need only one car, one apartment, one TV. Sharing expenses might even allow them to save some of their money. As they increase their incomes by advancing at their fast-food jobs, getting better jobs, or gaining more education, their opportunities and incomes will continue to grow.

Two people can share the workload at home, which becomes even more important when they have children. Two people often double the network of family and friends who can provide opportunities and assistance to the couple. And frankly, life is a lot more fun when you share it with someone in a committed, lifelong relationship. Two minds working together in marriage *can be* a tremendous benefit emotionally as well as financially.

"Can be" are the critical words in the last sentence. Today, nearly half of all marriages end in divorce. That's why Rule 3 has a second part, which is "stay married." Divorce is a nasty, costly event which can destroy all the hard-earned benefits you gain from living by the first and second rules. Divorce wastes money on lawyers, breaks apart households, disrupts the security of children, and often creates bitterness that lasts for many years.

This is the most difficult of the three rules because it is the only one that does not solely depend on you. This rule requires that you depend on a second person, your marriage partner, to hold to the rules as strongly as you do.

So how do you find a person whom you can love, and who will love and honor you through the difficult times every couple will face? How do you find a marriage partner who will stick with you to make it work?

For many years, I taught middle school and high school Sunday school classes. It amazed me to learn how most of my twelve- to eighteen-year-old students expected to find "the right one." They believed they would spot an attractive person of the opposite sex across the room, their eyes would meet, and they would instantly recognize each other as their one and only soul mate—with marriage, children, and happiness ever after soon to follow. Sorry, that's not how it works.

I spent a good deal of time in those classes introducing the idea of choosing a spouse on the basis of *character*. The biggest problem I found was that most of my students thought that they could change the "problem areas" in the other person *after* they got married. In most cases, this will not happen.

People are on their *best* behavior when dating. If you experience problem areas in the other person while dating, you need to decide if you can live with those problems, because they won't get better once you get married. They often get worse, a lot worse.

Money problems are the most common reason couples give for getting divorced, but money problems are usually the result of some other kind of irresponsible behavior. You need to be smart enough to be on the lookout for such behavior when you are dating. Watch how the other person handles money—do they overspend on cars, clothes, or other luxury items? Are they deeply in debt?

Do they have a gambling, drinking, or drug problem? How are their school and work habits? Is this a person you can count on to hold a job and contribute to the family income? Are they honest? Would you trust this person with your life? Remember, it isn't likely that their actions and behavior are going to improve after marriage.

Also look at their personal relationships. If your girlfriend or boyfriend can't get along with his or her own parents and family members, it is a warning sign. Those who can't control their emotions, and get into heated arguments with friends, teachers, employers and strangers create problems for everyone around them and aren't likely to have much success holding a job.

Another thing I learned about my students really surprised me: physical abuse between dating couples is much more common than I thought and seems to be increasing. Here is my advice to young ladies: *The first time a boyfriend hits you, leave, and never come back.* Any guy who uses physical force to get his way is too dumb to date you and will make your life miserable if you marry him. Don't fall for the line, "Sorry, I didn't mean it; it will never happen again." All physical abusers say that, but it's not true. It will only get worse; it always does. Get out while you still can.

A problem as big as physical abuse is *psychological abuse*, and it is carried out by boys against girls *and* by girls against boys.[43] If someone puts you down, embarrasses you in public, blames you for their bad behavior, threatens physical harm to you or your family, threatens suicide if you leave them, or uses other ways to discourage and undermine your confidence, you need to get out of that relationship.[44] Psychological abusers are often skilled at manipulating people's thoughts and feelings, undermining the confidence of their victims in order to control them.

If you find yourself in a physically or psychologically abusive marriage, you must take action to change the situation. It is not only your life that is at risk, but the life of any child in that relationship. Your abusing partner needs psychological help from experienced professionals. If your partner will not agree to treatment and commit to changing, *leave*, and take your children. This may result in breaking one of the rules I have asked you to keep, so this advice is not given lightly. Breaking one of the rules will always result in hardships, but here, you will have to weigh the hardships of staying in the relationship against the hardships of leaving for you and your children.

My advice to anyone thinking of marriage is, *take your time*. Don't rush. Don't set an illogical deadline, such as, "I have to get married by the end of high school or college, or before I'm 30." Concentrating on your education and job opportunities *before marriage* is the best way to avoid poverty and find a partner who will help provide a great life. If 50 percent of marriages end in divorce, you have a 50 percent chance of having to support yourself and your children on your own education and skills.[45]

Don't settle for less than you deserve—a person you want to be with for the rest of your life. It must be someone you can love and trust, someone you look forward to being with—not someone your parents think is best, or your friends say is perfect for you. It has to be the one *you* know is right for you.

If you are a person of faith, and I hope you are, it helps to find a marriage partner who understands and shares your beliefs.[46] The Bible has some interesting ideas on what to look for in a marriage partner. For men, see Proverbs 31:10–31 (The Wife of Noble Character) and First Corinthians 13:4–7. For women, see Titus 1:6–9 (Qualities of a Good Man) and First Corinthians 13:4–7. Then do this exercise: Write down the qualities you would really like and expect to find in a life partner. It will give you a guide to finding a good partner, and may quickly eliminate some candidates who only look good on the outside.

Once you complete your list, take a minute and look at yourself. Do *you* have the personal qualities you are looking for in a companion? Are *you* trustworthy, hard-working, and caring of others? Have *you* worked hard on your education? Do *you* get along with other people?

Can *you* contribute to the family finances like you should? You will best be able to choose a good marriage partner when you know you could live independently, on your own abilities, if you had to.

> **FOCUS ON BECOMING ALL OF THOSE THINGS YOU WANT TO FIND IN A MARRIAGE PARTNER, AND YOU WILL BE MORE LIKELY TO ATTRACT THAT KIND OF PERSON TO YOU.**

One more tip: Seek marriage counseling. Don't wait until your marriage is having big problems. Seek counseling up front, when you get engaged to be married. This is what my wife and I did, and it served us very well. Regardless of how well you think you know each other, professional counseling will bring up issues you may not have considered—finances, sharing household chores, child-rearing—and help you to resolve them *before* you get married. It will make those first years of marriage much easier because you've already talked about a lot of the issues new couples fight about.

What if you have already violated *all three* rules? You've gotten pregnant or gotten someone pregnant; you can't keep a job because of poor education, drug use or attitude; and you aren't married or you've already been divorced? Wow, you really are making it tough on yourself!

Can you still stay out of poverty? If you have broken all three rules you probably are living in poverty now or will at some point. You can still get out of poverty, but it will be much more difficult, and you have a lot of bad habits you will have to change, however, you are stronger than you think—you can still do this.

But what if you have taken on these rules as your own and accomplished them? Congratulations! You are on the road to capturing your dreams of a better life. You have already succeeded at overcoming some of the major obstacles to success. You have avoided the poverty trap. Now you have a good chance at making the leap to a life of prosperity for you and your family. Your hard work toward this better life will give your children a much safer and easier life as well.

Your children may never know how hard you had to work to achieve this, but you will see the results of your good efforts in their lives as well as your own. They will have better and safer lives with two responsible parents to care for them.[47] When you can afford to move your children to safer neighborhoods with better schools, you will give them a better chance at reaching the abundant life.

Your hard work, good character, and sacrifice will be a blessing to your children forever. You can be the one who breaks the curse of poverty for generations to come. Children follow their parents' example far more often than their parents' instructions. You can be that example.

YOU CAN DO THIS!

PART III: SMART

GROWING YOUR MIND

A RICH AND ABUNDANT LIFE:
THE HIGHER GOALS

A s I said before, I used to ask my Sunday school students every year what they wanted to learn, and discovered that they were interested in knowing the practical steps to living a rich and abundant life. I found, however, that it was much more difficult for my students to define a "rich and abundant life" than it was for them to define "poverty." They had a better understanding of what they wanted to avoid than what they wanted to achieve.

WHAT IS A RICH AND ABUNDANT LIFE?

What would your life be like if it was "rich and abundant"? "Rich" means you have money, you are affluent, well-off. "Abundant" means "plentiful." What would that kind of life look like to you?

When I first asked my students how much income they would need to live this better life I was surprised at how low they set their goals. Many originally thought that $30,000 a year would be enough. That is a pretty low target for a rich and abundant life, so we spent some time getting their goals up to a higher level. They all thought that having a family was an important part of achieving a great life, so they had to do some adjusting.

The median *family* income for Americans in 2013 was $51,939[48]. To be in the top 15 to 20 percent of Americans, you need an income of $100,000[49] or more per year. After thinking about it, my students decided that they wanted to be in that top 15 to 20 percent income bracket to support an abundant life. This is a good decision, because this high-income group is the fastest-growing segment of working Americans.[50]

But that is not all these students wanted. Here is a list of what they saw as necessary to live a rich and abundant life:

- A job they liked, at $100,000 or more per year
- A three-bedroom house with a pool—and no mortgage
- Plenty of nice clothes—and a walk-in closet for the house
- Car(s): Ford Mustangs and hot pick-up trucks seemed most popular—all paid for, of course
- Marriage: at their age, they were satisfied to be single, with marriage in the future
- Children: at some time in the future, but only after marriage (apparently I'd gotten through to them!)
- Family and Friends: loving family ties and good friends were important to them
- Faith: they wanted to build on their strong faith with a partner who had strong faith
- Health: not one of them mentioned health, but high school students believe they are ageless and indestructible—so I had to add "good health" myself.

I was really impressed that most of these young people seemed to realize that money and "stuff" were nice to have, and even important for a comfortable life, but they are not all there is to a good life. They understood that family, friends, love, and faith are important parts of a rich and abundant life.

And they are right—money never actually buys happiness. What money does give you is the great luxury of making choices. Poor people really have little control over their lives; their choices are very limited. A rich and abundant life includes having more possibilities to choose from.

Achieving a rich and abundant life is possible for most Americans, but again, there are a few simple rules you need to follow to achieve it. Like the first three rules, they are *simple but not easy*.

RULE ONE: WORK SMART

Work hard on your job, but work harder on improving yourself

T his is actually an expansion of Rule #2 in the Minimum Goals. What you learned there applies here as well, but it goes a little deeper. There are two parts to this rule; working hard on your job is the first part.

WHAT DOES "WORK SMART" REALLY MEAN?

Working smart on your job means learning what needs to be done and then *setting your own very high standards* for getting the job done.

As an example, if your father (or your boss) tells you to clean up the garage (or stockroom), you have a decision to make. You can decide to do *as little work as possible* (just sweeping the floor), or you can decide what a *first-class job*, one that will impress someone, would be. The difference is that doing as little as possible leaves your *dad* (or your *boss*) in charge of deciding how well you've done with the likely possibility of making you do more. But if you do the job to your own higher standard, it puts *you* in charge.

At one time in my life, it made me angry when someone asked me to do work. It made me feel like a lower-level person, a slave, and I resisted it. I used up all my energy doing the minimum, and I got angry if someone corrected me or made me do the work over again. There is a place for both anger and resistance, but not in the negative way I was using it. Negative anger and resistance eats up all your mental and physical energy.

When I was in seventh grade, my parents bought a small house with a garage. One of my chores was to keep the garage cleaned up, but I really didn't take responsibility for it—in other words, I never did it until I was told I had to.

Since the house was so small, a lot of things got stored in the garage— lawn equipment, tools, lumber, car parts, flower pots, golf clubs, sleds, furniture, rope, balls, ladders, and lots of other things. Because I had not accepted responsibility for this chore, it always came as a surprise when my dad said, "You need to clean up the garage today." It was always on a Saturday when I had something I wanted to do; there was never any prior notice, and it always irritated me.

None of that junk was mine—well, most of it wasn't—and I couldn't even drive yet, so why should I have to clear out a space for the car? I spent a lot of time trying to figure out the minimum amount of work required to pass my father's review. Most of the time it was less than he expected, resulting in more work, anger, and frustration.

One Saturday morning I was so angry about facing this job that I just sat down and moped in the garage. My mother came out and convinced me that this was not a good strategy, so I began thinking and came up with the idea of completely reversing the experience. I hadn't been given any guidelines for cleaning the garage, but that also meant I hadn't been given any limitations. I would do this to *my* standard. I would turn the whole thing on its head by *overdoing* the job.

I started by removing everything from the garage and putting it in the backyard. Two of my friends showed up and helped for a while, but they soon got tired and left to play baseball. I swept out the whole garage, then hosed the floor and swept out the water. Then I started putting things back, but I decided nothing would go on the floor; it would all have to be hung on the walls or placed on shelves. This was starting to become enjoyable because I was in charge and could organize the garage any way I wanted. It quickly became a game of "How much can I dazzle my dad?"

To store the lumber, I used some of the 2x4s to make a rack, which hung from the ceiling joists. I wall-mounted an old sheet of pegboard that became the area for hanging tools. When I ran out of metal pegboard hangers, I used some bent wire. Garden and lawn equipment went to one area and sports equipment to another.

When I finished hanging everything I considered worthy of space in *my* garage, there was a pretty good-sized pile of "junk" still in the yard, but I was out of hanger ideas and I had worked most of the day. I knew Dad would be coming home from work soon and I wanted the job to be done by the time he showed up to add to the "dazzle factor." So I moved all the rest of the junk to the back lot—and I burned it. Since there was so much junk to move, I recruited my friends back from the ball field— they were more than excited about getting to start a fire. I knew that if I didn't get rid of the junk, other family members might think these objects more worthy of storage and ruin my garage plan.

When my dad came home, he could not believe it. He just kept walking around in the garage, smiling and saying, "You did this all by yourself?" This was high praise. My mom was upset when she could not find an "antique" chair she thought was in the garage, but that was months later; and my brother was really mad when he found the charred remains of his broken hockey stick in the ashes on the back lot, but overall it was a great experience.

Oddly enough, I became rather protective of the garage and wouldn't let anyone mess it up. To my surprise, everyone else in the family gave in to my assumed authority. This, of course, kept the garage in good shape so I never again had to spend a Saturday cleaning it up. The difference was that I had taken responsibility for the chore, which also gave me the power to control my work.

When you TAKE responsibility, it GIVES you control.

It's interesting how things you dislike can become fun once you overcome your resistance and start using your brain to be creative. I learned that organizing a project takes more time up front, but saves loads of time in the future. And like any work, it helps to *make it a game*.

I discovered that if you set your own standard higher than others and do a better job than anyone expected, your work energy increases and the anger is replaced with enthusiasm. The drastic change this brings you is so positive and powerful it is almost hard to describe. It is the opposite of resisting the task. It is as if you were just waiting to do this job and the boss was holding you back—like you almost had to push him out of the way to get at it.

It can almost be intimidating to a boss when you take charge of a situation this strongly. It almost reverses the role of boss and employee. I can't quite explain the feeling—it's really exciting, and creates a confidence that you are becoming a person who can accomplish anything.

When you set your own high standards, you redirect your anger and resistance from what you *have to do* to what you *have chosen to do*—a better job than anyone else could do. The new attitude becomes, "I can do this better than anyone, and I'll prove it." That change in focus and attitude is frighteningly powerful, and because it is positive, it cannot be legitimately opposed.

POSITIVE SELF-DIRECTION

I didn't fully understand it at the time, but I had discovered the most basic and most important principle of success in life—positive self-direction. I had been able to change my anger (which was just a dumb reaction) into focus and energy. I was putting off the immediate fun of joining my friends for the delayed gratification of my dad's praise for doing something I had to do anyway. This ability to delay gratification—waiting for a bigger and better reward—is very important to a rich and abundant life.

Good employers want people who are willing to take charge. They want positive, self-directed people because managers are busy and don't want to waste time correcting the work of their employees. Good, reliable, take-charge employees are hard to find, so there will always be jobs for them—*always*—in good times and bad.

Because employers want to make sure they keep good workers, these are the employees who receive pay increases and promotions.

A good employer understands that a positive, self-directed employee knows what it takes to organize a job and get it done. A smart employer puts good employees like this into supervisory positions, in the hope that they can teach those skills to others. It's a double win, because the employer can now delegate work to the self-directed employee and give attention to other parts of the business.

Being put into a supervisory position is often the first big break for the positive, self-directed employee, but it is also a test, a moment of truth. Some positive, self-directed employees are great at doing their own work when they can control it all by themselves, but getting work done through others is a test of the employee's ability to organize and motivate people.

> **IF YOU CAN LEARN TO MANAGE THE WORK OF OTHERS IN A POSITIVE MANNER, YOUR FUTURE OPPORTUNITIES WILL BE ALMOST UNLIMITED.**

Learning this skill will allow your boss to give you more responsibility and place more authority under your capable control.

That is how good employers grow their businesses, and how you, a positive, self-directed employee, can get ahead in any career. It increases your pay and your experience at the same time. Employers pay more for increased skills and experience. This cycle of personal growth and development has always been here and always will be. It is a basic truth, a principle of life; it will never change.

If you have a boss who doesn't recognize your ability and reward you for it, find a new job—or start your own business and become your boss's competitor! This even works with fathers; if your dad doesn't recognize your good work, get a job with an employer who does, and maybe you won't be around the next time he needs the garage cleaned up.

IMPROVING YOURSELF—IN SCHOOL

The second part of this rule is to *work harder on improving yourself.* Your biggest opportunity to do this is with your education. Education in America is *free* all the way through high school; you have to attend anyway, so you may as well make it count. *The same principle we applied to the workplace can be applied to school.*

In the classroom, the teachers are in charge because they set the performance standards. But you don't have to let them have that power over you. Don't let the teachers set the standards. Set your own standards *and set them higher*. Truthfully, most teachers set the standards pretty low to account for the lazy students who aren't really trying, so this is not a hard game to win!

I've already warned you in the "Staying Out of Poverty" section of this book that people will try to get you to break your new rules. In school you may even find those people harder to deal with, because when you succeed in school you really will be showing some difference between you and everyone else. That will really upset those who aren't willing to work as hard as you or can't keep up. If you find that your "friends" are critical of you when you start working hard to learn and get good grades in school, you don't have very good friends. Believe me, this will happen. I know, because it happened to me.

When I started school, I had the misfortune of entering a public school system in Milwaukee, Wisconsin. At that time, the educators there were testing out a lot of new progressive education theories on the kids. These proved to be bad methods of teaching that they finally threw out, but by that time it was too late for me. I missed some of the important basics in reading, writing, and spelling.

It wasn't all the fault of the teachers, however. I had undiagnosed learning disabilities too, but adding my own difficulties to the school system's experiments in teaching put me in a difficult position. The fact that we moved multiple times didn't help, either. By the time I graduated from high school, I had gone to nine different schools.

When my family moved to a new and better school system in Illinois, I found myself far behind the other kids in my grade. My fifth grade teacher, Mrs. Helger, told me I would never be able to go to college because of my bad grades and poor academic abilities. That's a very discouraging thing to hear from your teacher, and the worst part was

I believed it. I was too ashamed to talk to my parents about it; they seemed smart to me, so I figured they already knew I was not smart. I didn't think there was a way out.

When I was in middle school, our family moved again, and I was in an even better school system in Indiana, which only put me further behind all the other kids. I thought I was the dumbest kid in the class, and I hated school. I remember watching the clock, and how the minutes seemed to drag on for hours during the endless school day. There was nothing to save me from the hated embarrassment of failing in every subject—except art, but that wasn't an academic subject, so it didn't seem to count.

As eighth grade ground down slowly toward its end in spring, the teachers started talking about our move to high school the next year. They said there was a new Indiana state test, which would be given at the end of the eighth grade year for placement in high school. I was particularly bad at taking timed tests, but there was no avoiding it. I took the test and forgot about it. After all, they said it wasn't a pass/fail, graded test. They couldn't keep you from going on to high school—not in America, could they?

As school let out for the summer, it occurred to me that high school was a chance to start all over again. The high school teachers wouldn't know I was the "dumbest" kid in the class. I wondered what would happen if I really organized myself and made every effort to get good grades, right from the first day. I knew from my older brother that they didn't have "spelling bees" and other nonsense like that in high school; they based your grades on the tests you took on the material. You had a different teacher for every class, so if you were stupid in one subject, the teacher in the next class might not even know it. The more I thought about it, the more it seemed like there might be a way to pull this off.

For the first time in my life I committed to a difficult goal: I would make straight As in high school. I would do *anything and everything* it took to reach this goal. I was sick and tired of being the dumbest kid, and I was determined to change that fact. I told absolutely no one about this goal. It was my secret objective. I would surprise them—no,

I would "dazzle" them—with my abilities. This was beginning to sound exciting to me. I would make it a game, and I would win before anyone knew the game was on.

I had a job that summer, but in my spare time, I started reading books—something I had never done before. It was the only thing I could think of that might help prepare me in some way to achieve my secret goal. At a neighbor's yard sale I found a box of old books. When the neighbor saw I was interested in reading, he sold me the whole box for a dollar.

The box was filled with great classics like *The Adventures of Tom Sawyer*, *Around the World in 80 Days*, *A Tale of Two Cities*, *Treasure Island*, *To Kill a Mockingbird*, *The Call of the Wild*, *Brave New World*, and *Twenty Thousand Leagues Under the Sea*. It was slow going at first because I wasn't a fast reader, but I really enjoyed those great books. Plowing through those books really improved my reading ability and quickly expanded my vocabulary. My parents started thinking I was weird, and even asked my older brother, "Why is he always reading books instead of going out with his friends?" Something was changing, but since it wasn't negative, they weren't really worried, just confused. I loved it.

I also thought about what I could do in high school to stand out from the crowd in the eyes of the teachers I would be trying to impress. Everyone wore jeans to school; I decided I would only wear khakis, like college kids wore. College kids were the ones who had done well in high school, so looking like them might help. When my one pair of khakis started to fray and I refused to wear jeans, my mother finally bought me another pair. I never wore a pair of jeans to high school.

My older brother, who had been a high school football star, told me that the football coach taught the required freshman health classes, and gave an A to everyone on the football team. I was not a star athlete in any sport: I was five foot six, 134 pounds, and nearsighted. But I signed up for football before school started. That was a guaranteed A in one class—whatever it took, *anything and everything!*

RULE ONE: WORK SMART

When high school started, I was excited, because I had a plan. I knew no one else had a plan—this was just high school. My first class was freshman biology. I looked around and didn't recognize a single person in class. Our high school consolidated all of the students from three middle schools, but still, this was a small town; I should have recognized somebody. I noticed right away that the kids were a pretty unruly bunch, and the teacher had difficulty getting control of the class. This seemed odd to me, and it was the same in my second and third classes.

My first class after lunch was homeroom. My homeroom teacher explained that, for the first time, students had been divided into three groups based on the placement tests we had all taken at the end of eighth grade. The first group was college preparation, the second group was junior/technical college preparation, and the third group was high school completion. I was stunned.

It was obvious to me that I had been placed in the last group—the group they didn't think would make it through high school. My plan had been based on a fresh start, a clean slate, anonymity—on the teachers not knowing I was "that dumb kid" from grade school. How could they do this to me? I was defeated by "the system" before I even had a chance!

I labored through the last two afternoon classes, went to football practice, got my tail kicked by some very large varsity linemen and then walked home. Not a good day! As I walked I got angry, but then I decided to calm down and focus on the problem.

By the time I reached home, I had come up with a new plan. It occurred to me that being in the lowest level group could be an advantage. After all, the kids in that group really weren't trying very hard, and the teacher probably graded on a curve; I could stand out more easily against these kids. I studied until 11:30 that night, rewriting and organizing all the notes I had taken in class that day and reading ahead in two classes. My new plan was to double down on my old plan and to be aggressive with it. They could throw every lousy obstacle they had at me and I would still beat them.

63

I almost ran to school the next morning. In every class, I raised my hand every time the teacher asked a question because I knew the answers. This is considered bad manners in high school—"sucking up." I didn't care. I wasn't there to win friends; I was there to achieve my *one goal*. A couple of kids hassled me about showing off to the teachers. My response was to stand up the next time I raised my hand. I didn't do this once or twice; I did this every day, for every question, in every class. Teachers started saying, "Does anyone besides Segal know the answer?" Cool!

It seemed that my plan was working, and I was determined to stick with it. Not once was I late for class, and I studied (no talking) during study hall. In my mind, this was my last chance. I didn't care if it caused me to lose every friend I had. It's good that I had totally committed to my plan, because that is exactly what happened.

My friends decided that I didn't want their friendship anymore because all I did was study—until 11:00 or 12:00 every night and all weekend long, except Saturday night. I had made a commitment to something more important to me than spending time with them, and they interpreted this as a rejection of their friendship. I didn't intend it that way, but that is what happened. I actually tried to explain it to my best friend, but he wasn't doing well in school and it made him angry. In the second half of my freshman year, I began to make new friends, but they were a completely different group—all high-performing students. All my old friends had disappeared, and they would never return, no matter how much I tried to be friendly to them.

Twice, a teacher made a mistake in class regarding some fact I knew was wrong. In both cases, I immediately raised my hand and loudly corrected them. This was intimidating to the teacher, of course, just as I intended it to be. You would think that this might be contrary to my objective of standing out in a positive way to the teachers, but things were changing.

After some initial hostility and bullying, the other kids in my low-level classes started to see me in a different light. They realized that the placement tests had cast them down into the basement of low achievers, just as they had done for me. The other students seemed sort of proud that someone in their group could answer all the questions and even confront the teachers with knowledge. They seemed to respect the fact that I wouldn't back down for anyone. The low-level classrooms settled down and a few of the kids even seemed to be trying. When you go against the crowd, the first thing you get is resistance and bullying—but if you stick to it, you start to get followers.

My confidence was growing, and I had won enough respect from the teachers that there were no negative consequences from my corrections. I was discovering the power of being highly prepared; of proving that I could perform to the highest standard—and that standard was my own.

Report cards were handed out four times a year in homeroom, at the middle and at the end of each semester. Students had to return them the next day with their parent's signature. I stuck mine in a book without looking at it and pretended to be reading, as if I didn't have any concern or even interest in opening the envelope to check the grades. Everyone else had immediately done that.

I kept "reading" as everyone left the class because I knew others would ask how I had done. I was afraid to look. Had my plan really worked, or was I about to be crushed one more time?

As I started to leave, my homeroom teacher said, "Hey, you really did well. I'm proud of you." But even this didn't quell my fears because "doing well" compared to how I had done in grade school could have meant Bs and Cs. I went to the boy's bathroom, entered a stall, closed the door, and opened the envelope. Straight As. Tears came to my eyes. I had done it. I knew I had the power to change my life. The bell rang. I would be late for class for the first time. I didn't care. I was going to enjoy this moment.

One afternoon, toward the end of the second grading period, I was called to the principal's office. I had never been called to the principal's office before. But I had just been elected to the student council the previous week. As the sole representative from the lowly "high school completion" level, I thought maybe he wanted to congratulate me.

Claude Krump had been the high school principal for thirty-four years. Upperclassmen called him "Slider" because he had a weird sort of shuffle when he walked. Of course, no student ever used this demeaning nickname in the presence of any adult.

When I got to the office, the ancient school secretary motioned me into Mr. Krump's office without looking up from her card file. The principal's office door was open so I stepped a cautious two feet inside and stopped. "You wanted to see me, Mr. Krump?"

He never asked me to sit down. "Segal, what did you do on those eighth grade placement tests to mess them up?"

I said, "I don't know what you mean. I just took the test like everybody else."

"Well, I don't think so. You must have meant to mess them up, as low as they were, and they just don't correlate with the grades you're making in high school. You weren't trying at all on that test, and it makes the whole thing look like we didn't do it right. I don't know if you thought it was a big joke to sandbag that test, but no one else is laughing. The testing people in Indianapolis say we made big mistakes, and yours is the biggest one they point to. So you're going to take it over again, and this time you're going to take it serious, by God."

I couldn't believe what I was hearing. I told Mr. Krump I didn't understand, but he just rattled on, pretty much repeating the same thing. They wanted me to take the eighth grade placement test over because the results were so far off from my performance in high school—after I was already *in* high school? Then he said, "You take the test over, and take it serious this time. I'm sure the results will show where you're supposed to be, and we can move your placement up to the top group. Then this thing will correlate like it's supposed to and everybody will be happy. I'm sure you'd like to move up to the higher placement group." As I reflect on that day, it was an important moment in my life—my first lesson in bureaucratic stupidity.

The idea of having to take that test again scared me to death. I didn't want to move anywhere. I was a stand-out right where I was. I knew that my school performance was due to my hard work, relentless study, and changed attitude. My high school tests were based on the course material I was mastering. I knew that I wouldn't be any better at taking a general academic placement test than I was a year before in eighth grade. The straight As were based on my organization and study—the fruits of my secret plan.

I could hardly believe it myself, but I said, "No, sir."

Mr. Krump was always red in the face in the afternoons, but he got much redder and his whole face seemed to expand like a balloon. "What do you mean, no? You be up here in the side office at 8:30 Monday morning ready to take that test and apply yourself, young man. Do you hear me?"

"Yes, sir," I said. "I'll come up here at 8:30 if I'm called out of class, and I'll sit in the side office, but I won't take the test again."

It was as if he didn't hear what I said. "Well, yes, you be up here at 8:30 just like I told you and we'll get this thing behind you. Now get back to class and don't linger in the hallway." This time as I passed through the outer office, the secretary wasn't looking at her card file. She was wide-eyed, and she was looking right at me.

At our high school, students didn't say "no" to the high school principal for any reason, particularly freshmen. I really wasn't the confrontational type, but I hated the idea of taking a general aptitude test again and failing in the eyes of teachers, testers, and myself. It was all so pointless. Why couldn't they just be satisfied that I was doing well in school? Wasn't that what they were there for? If I took the stupid test again and did just as poorly—a likely result—they would just think I sabotaged the test again. There was no way to win this by taking that test again.

I had the courage to say "no" because I was scared. My secret plan was working, and I couldn't take the chance of exposing it or having to justify it. I didn't want to "blow my cover." At the time, it seemed to me that it might destroy the power and effectiveness of my plan. I relished the fact that I had blindsided them—had come out of nowhere like superman and blazed to the top of the heap, confounding their lousy placement test in the process.

As I walked home that evening, my new confidence began to kick in. I knew that I was no longer considered dumb by teachers or other students in high school. In fact, I was considered to be one of the smart kids, and I had the grades to prove it. They really couldn't force me to take the test if I just sat there, and they really couldn't justify making me take it again. I thought, "I've got them." This was just like catching one of my teachers in a factual error, and I wasn't about to let it go. I was ready to shout "NO!" from the rooftops.

I admit I was a little scared the following Monday morning, but I was also excited about confronting them again. I would be polite, but I would refuse to do what they had no right or reason to make me do. What could they do, make me go back to eighth grade after I had made straight As for almost a full semester in high school? That thought was so ridiculous I laughed out loud.

I went to my 8 o'clock class and waited for the call, but the first period passed without a summons from the principal. I avoided passing by the principal's office for the entire week, but still, there was no demand to appear. No one ever mentioned it again.

When I went to my first class at the beginning of the second semester, it was filled with the best students in the high school freshman class. I had been quietly placed in the top group. Schoolwork never became easy for me like it did for many of those kids. It always seemed to take a lot more work on my part to make good grades, but I was willing to do that because that was my "secret" plan.

Setting that *one goal* and dedicating myself to achieving it had worked better than I ever imagined. It changed my life forever—because *I* had changed.

HOW MUCH EDUCATION SHOULD YOU GET?

I remember one of my grade school teachers asking each person in class to stand up and say what they wanted to be when they grew up. My classmates said they wanted to be firemen or nurses or farmers or police officers. When it came to me, I stood up and said, "I want to be rich." This got a pretty good laugh from my classmates, of course, but the truth was, I just had a very healthy fear of being poor. The teacher said, "Well, what kind of work would you like to do to get rich?" I said that I guess I would like to be a businessman. It always seemed to me that people who had some kind of business lived better than other people and I liked the idea of being my own boss.

Because I had worked hard at changing myself in high school, I was able to get into Indiana University, where I earned a degree in Business Management. And because I was in the Reserve Officers Training Course (ROTC) program, I was also commissioned as an officer in the Army when I graduated from college.

Being an officer opened up new opportunities for me. I was told I could delay my active duty service if I went on to get a graduate degree—and they would *pay* me while I went to school! This deal was too good to pass up.

Getting a graduate degree was never a goal of mine until my senior year in college, when I took a required course in business law. This was considered one of the tougher courses in the business department, but I loved the class, got an A, and decided that I would try to get into law school. The law school entrance exam (LSAT) was a big concern, but I managed to pass that hurdle and was accepted into the freshman law class at Indiana University. I started my studies immediately that summer and graduated two and a half years later with a Juris Doctorate (JD) degree in law. I passed the bar exam and was legally qualified to practice law in the great State of Indiana.

Back in grade school I never could have imagined that I would be capable of getting into law school. No one else could have imagined it either. I only wish my fifth grade teacher, Mrs. Helger, who told me I could not go to college, could have been there to see me graduate with a law degree. She would have been even more surprised to see me teach a class to Law/MBA joint degree graduate students at Indiana University many years later.

I can't tell you how much formal education you need. It depends on your goals in life, your desire and ability to do school work, and how you want to earn a living. High school graduation is essential; you have to get solid basic abilities in reading, writing, and math. You also need to know basic computer skills. But there are many very good jobs and career paths that don't require a four-year college degree. For many people, getting experience or a trade school degree in a basic skill like welding, auto repair, nursing, construction, electronics, or computers is a better way to go. It is less expensive and takes less time to graduate.

Studies show that getting a degree from a community college after high school increases your chances of moving up from the lowest quarter of income earners by 30 percent[51] and adds an average of $7,900 a year more to your income than someone with a high school diploma.[52] Over a forty-year career, that adds up to $316,000, which is a good incentive to attend community college and graduate. If you earn a degree in a high-demand area like computer science, engineering or health care, this added income is much higher.[53] More formal education generally results in more lifetime income.

If you decide to get a technical degree first, and want to get more formal education later, those job skills can help support you. Even if you don't go beyond a high school education, basic job skills in your areas of interest can offer possibilities for advancement and future business opportunities.

The Millionaire Next Door[54], by Tom Stanley and William Danko, is a terrific book showing that most American millionaires don't inherit their money. More than 80 percent *earned* their money, mostly by starting small businesses in things like construction, plumbing, and excavation. They don't look like millionaires, because they drive pickup trucks that they use for their work and put most of their money back into their businesses to build assets.[55]

School advisors say you should find your passion and follow a career in something you love to do. The catchphrase is "If you make a career out of something you love to do, you'll never work a day in your life." The problem for me was that no one seemed interested in paying me much money for the things I loved to do. So I went into the tool manufacturing business with my brother.

Manufacturing industrial cutting tools wasn't something we had always aspired to; it wasn't something my brother and I dreamed about as children. But it was a good business opportunity. We liked business in general, and we learned to like the tool manufacturing business once we got good at it. As we learned to make the business more profitable, we really started to like it.

Once you get interested in something difficult and become really good at it, you often learn to enjoy it, and people are more likely to pay you well for doing difficult things with excellence. At least that is my experience. I think that too many young people don't ever commit to a career path because they haven't found their "passion." They jump from one thing to another and eventually run out of time.

If you decide to attend college, the type of degree you get is, in most cases, more important to your future income than the national ranking of your college. Where you went to school can make a difference in getting your first job, but after that, your personal performance will mean more than your alma mater. Go after a career that will give you *job opportunities* when you graduate. Before you decide on a career, investigate the job opportunities in that field at your public library and on the Internet. Talk to some people who have college degrees and work in the same type of job you want to get after graduation. This will be your best source of information about the kinds of careers that can give you the type of future you want.

Do your best to stay away from college debt. It is better to take a year off and work to earn money for the next year's education costs than to get buried under a mountain of debt before you even get a job. Enlisting in the military can be helpful if you aren't sure what career you want. Every branch of the military will open doors to many other opportunities, career ideas and money for college.

During the first year I was in the Army, our group was assigned the task of creating a brand new air defense unit. We recruited and trained all the personnel. They were young men right out of high school with few abilities and no experience. But after months of training they developed skills and started to get excited about passing the unit qualification field tests. Our final test was three days of firing *live* surface-to-air missiles at Air Force fighter jets which dragged high-heat elements on wire tethers behind the jets as they flew. When fired, our heat-seeking missiles were supposed to destroy the high-heat elements rather than the jets—if everything went right.

As OIC (Officer In Charge) of the three days of testing at the White Sands Missile Range, I was more than a little nervous about how our young guys would perform under pressure. There were hundreds of civilians and at least two Congressmen observing these tests. Once I gave the "weapons free" order, all the action depended on the privates and sergeants—most of them *teenagers*—whom we had trained. They all performed without a single error and we qualified. I was so proud of them. They had accepted the challenge, developing confidence and character as well as skills and experience.

The military not only provides money for education, they give young people huge amounts of training, responsibility, and opportunity; experiences that build confidence and skills you can use for the rest of your life.

WORK EXPERIENCE: EDUCATION WITH INCOME

Working at a job can be the best learning experience you ever have. You can start this kind of learning at a very young age. There are all kinds of summer jobs and part-time work you can find if you are willing to start at the bottom and work your way up. If you view these early work experiences as education to build your skills rather than just a job, it will help you to see future opportunities. Even work around the house—like my experience with cleaning the garage—can help you learn to organize and complete a project. Seeing work as a chance to learn and grow makes all the difference.

Brad is a friend of mine who had the ability, but not the desire, to go to college. While he was still in high school, he agreed to cut a neighbor's lawn in exchange for an old car. His neighbor was experienced in building construction and repair work, and often took Brad along with him to job sites since Brad was interested in learning all about this type of work. All through high school, Brad helped his neighbor at these construction jobs for little or no pay. He looked at this work as a chance to learn about something he wanted to do in the future.

Brad's neighbor is what you call a *mentor*—a person who is knowledgeable and experienced in something you want to learn, and is willing to help and guide you in learning. Those who are good at something usually love to talk about it, and are often very willing to help a young person by mentoring them. If you know someone who is good at what you want to learn, talk to them; very likely, they will be glad to help you.

Brad had made good grades in school, but he told me, "After high school, I just didn't want to go to school any more. I wanted to get out and start working on my own." He bought the neighbor's lawn mower and started cutting lawns for many other people. He then got a contract with his church to cut the grass in their large cemetery. At first he didn't know anything about small engine repair, but when the lawn mower broke down, Brad had to learn about it—fast.

When the cemetery's gravedigger left town, Brad got a contract with the church to take over the grave digging. He rented a backhoe for the job, and did a lot of hand shoveling as well. The next summer he had saved enough to buy a used backhoe; a few months later, he had saved enough to buy a used dump truck to haul the extra dirt.

In a few years he had plenty of work during the summer when the grass grew, but not much in the winter. He continued to save most of his profits because he wanted to grow his business without having to make loans and go into debt. This paid off a few years later when a local man wanted to sell his small business. Brad bought the business, which had several used trucks with plow blades; the former owner had used the trucks to plow snow in the winter. Brad contracted with local businesses to plow their parking lots in the winter. He hired his younger brother to help with the snow removal and dirt hauling. When there was heavy snow, he and his brother would sometimes have to plow for thirty hours straight to get all of the work done. He bought another used riding mower and hired two guys to cut the lawns. The next spring his employees cut the lawns, and he used the backhoe and trucks for some landscaping jobs. The following year he started digging and repairing drainage pipe ditches for local contractors.

In his spare time, Brad purchased a piece of land in the country with a lake. He built himself a small house on the property, getting help from friends in the construction businesses he was servicing with his digging and hauling equipment. Brad is now married with three children living in that house. Last year he built a large pole barn to house his bulldozer, backhoes, dump trucks, lawnmowers, and other equipment. The building also has an equipment maintenance and repair area. He is growing his business by reinvesting his profits rather than borrowing money from a bank.

The used equipment which my friend bought is what people in business call *capital equipment*, because he uses it to do work, which generates a profit. This is where the term *capitalism* comes from. Free-market capitalism allows a person to start their own small business and grow it using the profits they earn. It is the system that has created *all* the wealth in America. It is a system you can use to become as wealthy as you want—if you are smart enough to see the opportunities and are willing to work very hard to turn those opportunities into reality.

My friend now has a business of his own, which he can grow to any size he wants. His business has given him a wide knowledge about equipment repairs, accounting, hiring employees, excavating, payroll, cash management, landscaping, bill collecting, scheduling, sales, writing contracts, real estate, and many other areas. He developed his broad knowledge, like his capital equipment, a little at a time. He has acquired *work-hardened knowledge* because the mistakes he made along the way resulted in costs right out of his own pocket, just as his successes put money into his pocket. Brad's story is one of hard work and success, but, in America, there are many other stories like his.

Tom and his wife, Juanita, live in the same town as Brad. They have a thriving pool supply business, but that is not how they started; in fact, they started with nothing. Tom grew up on a farm. At age fourteen he had a job at a gas station in the summer and after school in the winter.

After graduating from high school he got a job working in a small auto body repair shop. A few years later the owner of the body shop wanted to get out of the business, so he sold it to Tom for a few thousand dollars. Tom worked hard and paid off the debt to the previous owner. He now had his own small, debt-free business. His wife, Juanita, also had her own small business as a hairdresser, operating out of their house.

There was a lawn and garden business next to Tom's auto body repair shop, and Tom started repairing lawn mowers and other small engines for that business. He found that he liked the lawn and garden business more than the auto business, so he sold his body shop and started working in the lawn and garden business. Soon he was working all available hours of the day trimming trees, planting shrubs, and doing all kinds of landscaping. This was Tom's second small business.

Tom and his wife had several children by this time and they decided to build a pool in their backyard. After contacting several companies for quotes, Tom realized he was not satisfied with the pool vendors he had dealt with, and thought this might be another business opportunity. Tom and Juanita decided to start a pool supply business. They tore down an old barn on their property and put up a pole shed to store inventory for the new business. They used the knowledge they had from servicing their own pool and studied other information to find suppliers for the new business.

Tom and Juanita offered pool servicing and pool supplies. In time the business grew and they ran out of space in the pole shed. They bought an old restaurant building in a good location, remodeled it, and moved in. The added space allowed them to add grills, lawn and pool furniture, playground equipment, and many other items to their pool supplies. They were growing the business by offering new products which they knew their customers wanted.

Successful businesses are created when someone sees a needed product or service and works to fill that need. And we can use our own interests and talents to provide those products—like Landy.

Landy liked to bake from the time she was little. Her older sister decided to open a coffee shop in their small town. This was long before coffee shops were popular, so her sister took her to the big city—Indianapolis—to see one. Her big sister had the idea of offering fresh muffins with the coffee. She did not love baking like Landy, so she bought a muffin recipe from someone who was selling a lot of muffins in the city.

The night before the grand opening of the coffee shop, Landy's sister finally had the bakery oven in place and tested the recipe—the muffins were awful. In a panic, she called Landy, the one who did love baking. Landy stayed up all night to produce delicious blueberry muffins for the grand opening.

At that time, Landy had two small children at home, but she started coming to the coffee shop early in the morning, before the kids woke up, to bake the muffins. She developed a whole line of blueberry, banana, nut, chocolate, and cranberry muffins. Her sister paid her based on the number of muffins sold.

A few years later, Landy's sister decided to sell the business. There were no immediate buyers so someone suggested Landy should buy the coffee shop. "It had never occurred to me that I could own or run my own business," Landy said. "I didn't know if I was smart enough." But she found the means to buy half the business, and her mother bought the other half. Over time, Landy bought out her mother's half of the business, as she had promised.

Landy decided to buy the building in which the coffee shop is located, rather than continuing to pay rent. This made the building a *capital investment* for Landy, rather than a rental expense. Instead of paying rent she is now paying off a mortgage, which will allow her to own the building in a few years. She also added a complete line of health products to the offering, as well as great lunches. "We got the idea of adding fresh lunch salads because that is what all of us working at the coffee shop wanted for lunch and there was no place in town to get what we wanted." Landy still comes in before the sun rises every morning to bake muffins and prepare lunches. She works many hours each day and doesn't take vacations. The coffee shop is busy and growing—and the muffins are fantastic!

Each of these three small business owners graduated from high school but did not go on to college. They did not start out knowing how to do all the things needed to create and manage a business. They just did the work and learned what they had to learn to survive one day at a time. They were smart enough to take action when an idea or an opportunity presented itself.

Not everything they tried worked, but most things did. They often talked to, and learned from, other people who could help them learn about business, and they learned by trial and error. The most important thing is that they refused to stop learning and challenging themselves. They have all kept working, growing and learning.

> FORMAL EDUCATION WILL MAKE YOU A LIVING;
> SELF-EDUCATION CAN MAKE YOU A FORTUNE
> Jim Rohn

This is the promise that a free enterprise system offers those who are willing to take the risk and do the work. Free enterprise, which allows people from all walks of life to prosper by providing goods and services to others, is the only system that allows people to do this. It is also the only system that works. It allows people who start out with little or nothing to work and improve their lives. It is a system worth cherishing and protecting.

The biggest advantage that these entrepreneurs have created for themselves is that they have a profitable business with *capital value*. They get income from the business, which they use for living expenses, but they reinvest most of those profits back into maintaining and growing the business. They are building business *assets* which they will be able to sell at some time in the future if they want to retire or do something else with their lives. And since they own their own businesses, they have more direct control of their work life and income. They may not become wealthy, and that may not be their objective, but the knowledge and experience they accumulate through their efforts is a great value that they will always possess.

Many of their friends did go to college or into the military, and have returned to take jobs in the community. Some of their friends probably earn more take-home pay than these small business owners, but there is a difference. Their friends' jobs are subject to outside forces (such as the merger or sale of their employer's business) that could end or seriously affect their jobs. Also, their friends have a job and a salary, but they are not yet building any business capital assets. They may be earning more money each year but small business owners have the added ability to accumulate wealth (value) in their businesses.

Their college-educated friends may be able to rise in their companies and one day may even own stock (a capital asset) in that company or they may start a business, write books, invest in stocks, patent inventions, or create some other kind of capital asset to increase their future income. But if they don't, I will guarantee you that my friends who started these small businesses—mowing lawns, hauling dirt, fixing pools, baking muffins—will have more wealth and security, through the tremendously challenging work of owning and controlling their own businesses.

> **WORKING ON YOUR JOB WILL EARN YOU A SALARY. WORKING ON IMPROVING YOURSELF WILL BRING YOU ABUNDANCE.**

At first, you may have to take a low-level job where there isn't much you can learn. If this is the case, keep looking for a way to move up in the place you are working and keep looking for better employment opportunities where you can learn. Don't quit your old job until you have a solid opportunity at a better job. It is always easier to find a better job while you are employed.

How you focus your learning makes a difference. If you can become interested in learning things you can use in your work, you will become much more successful. Every job, every type of work—is *work!* Even if you like your job, there will be parts of it that are not fun. If you can find a way to eliminate parts of your work which you don't like, or learn how to do them well, they will no longer be a problem.

In some cases, mastering the things you don't like will change them into things you are good at and like to do. Once you master them, you have developed unique talent and insight. What you once saw as nearly impossible becomes routine, even simple. Others will take notice. Your ability to succeed and your confidence to handle anything in life rapidly expands. **Many new products and companies have been built by people who found ways to eliminate or simplify jobs no one likes to do.**

SMALL HABITS, BIG RESULTS

"An apple a day keeps the doctor away." You have heard that one before, haven't you? Well, what if it were true? A broader interpretation of this old adage would be that if you eat healthy food and stay away from sweets and other "junk" food, you would be so healthy you wouldn't ever have to go to the doctor. If that were true, do you think that most people would actually do it?

Even if there were a single, simple daily action that would protect one's health, I don't think most people would practice it, because it would require discipline. All you have to do is look around you to see large health problems resulting from a small lack of discipline.

Studies show that 65 percent of Americans are overweight, and 33 percent are not just overweight, but obese.[56] While eating one apple a day won't insure you will never be sick, we know without any doubt that it is healthier than eating a candy bar and drinking a soda every day, but most Americans eat the candy and drink the soda. Why? Because most people don't think that these small habits really make any difference. *They don't want to think about the long-term result.*

Less than half of Americans exercise regularly (defined as three times per week for at least thirty minutes) and that number is declining. The Gallup-Healthways Well-Being Index measures five elements of well-being for Americans: purpose in life, social well-being, financial stability, community involvement, and physical health. Their findings show that being overweight not only causes health problems, but that obesity is also linked to lower social well-being, lower income, longer unemployment, and overall lower financial well-being.[57]

But doesn't living a rich and abundant life mean eating and drinking as much as you want? Not for long, it doesn't. Being overweight and out of shape aren't part of the better life you want. Two things will determine how healthy you are in your lifetime: your genetics (the genes you inherited from your parents), and your weight. You can't do much about your genetics, but you are totally in control of your weight, and you must stay in control of it if you are going to live a rich and abundant life. What good is abundance in money, work and earning power, a good family and marriage, a great house, cars, clothes and everything else if you are physically sick and declining? In order to *enjoy* abundance you have to develop lifestyle habits which keep you healthy enough to benefit from it.

You can go overboard in the other direction, of course. You don't need to be as skinny as a supermodel. That can be just as unhealthy. Set a healthy target weight and adjust your eating and exercise to maintain it. The abundant life comes from understanding how to balance all aspects of your life; it is less about how you look and more about how you feel.

When I asked my Sunday school class to describe a rich and abundant life, they didn't even think about listing good health; I had to add that one for them. That is because they were young. Most people don't think about their health at an early age because most of us are healthy when we are young.

When we are young, our metabolism runs at a faster pace, burning more calories, and we tend to get more exercise from walking or riding a bike to get around. But as we age, our metabolism starts to slow down and we trade the walking and biking for driving and riding. Too many adults stop being physically active and eventually become couch potatoes. Unfortunately, dramatic increases in child obesity indicate that this sedentary life style is being chosen earlier in life. We have all become aware of the growing problem of childhood obesity.[58] This is a bad choice you don't have to make.

I wasn't much of an athlete in high school. I wasn't a fast runner, I was nearsighted, and I wasn't big enough for football or tall enough for basketball. Physical fitness had never been part of my life until I was required to get in shape by the Army. Drill sergeants can be very persuasive.

During the summer after sophomore year, ROTC students had to go to Army boot camp for six weeks. This was required if we wanted to complete the last two years of the program and get commissioned as second lieutenants. The ROTC cadets from Indiana University were sent to Fort Riley—a hot, humid, flat, dry, treeless military camp near Junction City, Kansas. To prepare for it, in the spring prior to boot camp, we started running. To qualify for summer camp, we had to run at least two miles in eighteen minutes wearing combat boots. It was the first time I ever tried to get in shape. By the end of boot camp I was *really* in shape for the first time in my life, and I felt great!

I actually started to enjoy running. In fact, I liked it so much that I still run three to five miles at least three times a week. It wasn't the running itself that hooked me on exercise, it was the strong healthy feeling I had after I finished. Runners refer to it as the "endorphin high." I also felt a new mental alertness along with the physical fitness. I continued this during my work career, even when I was traveling, because the benefits I felt were so great.

> IT IS THE SMALL HABITS WE BUILD
> INTO OUR LIVES WHICH MAKE THE
> BIGGEST DIFFERENCE.

Physical fitness became a habit for me. The hardest part of running every day wasn't the running itself; it was getting out of bed early in the morning to go out into the summer heat or winter cold. Overcoming the challenge of that small obstacle every day provided a fantastic kick-start to the day, and a boost to my confidence, mental clarity, and physical energy. To get out of poverty and into the middle class and beyond, you will need to maintain strong mental and physical energy.

If you don't like running, there are plenty of other inexpensive ways to stay in shape. It's good to join a gym if you can afford it, but walking, riding a bike, running, playing tennis, joining a dance class, and many other activities are great for staying in shape. Do something you enjoy and it will be easier to stay motivated. Whatever you do, make it part of your daily routine. Get hooked on the positive habit of exercise.

And that's what it needs to be—a *habit*—something you build into your weekly schedule. Don't be a "binge" exerciser, the way some people are binge eaters and drinkers. Binge exercisers pack the gyms and workout rooms every January because they made a New Year's resolution after eating too much in December. The gyms and workout rooms are usually back to normal by the middle of February because the bingers don't stick with it. Habits are slower, steadier, more committed and more effective, because they last. If you want to understand more about eliminating bad habits and reinforcing good habits, read *The Power of Habit* by Charles Duhigg.[59]

Physical fitness is only one of the positive habits you can build into your life. Reading is another. Regularly reading high quality books and articles not only develops your reading skills, it increases your knowledge, improves your writing skills, and expands your vocabulary.

Using good grammar in normal conversation is an important habit, and it is *expected* in the workplace today. Poor grammar can cause you great damage by making you sound uneducated. Employers will hesitate to promote an employee who sounds uneducated when speaking to a customer.

Personal hygiene—being clean and neat—are basic and expected in any workplace. These are habits you can and should start at an early age; and, you can dress modestly and appropriately for the job at very little cost. You want your boss and co-workers to focus on your abilities, not your appearance.

These are subtle things, but people notice them. It is politically correct these days to say that such things don't make a difference, that we should judge people on how they perform, not on how they look or act, but that's nonsense. You are judged on the whole package you present. If you are so out of shape you can't get around, you use bad grammar in business meetings and in front of customers, you stumble reading adult-level text, you write and spell poorly, and you can't do basic math, it *will* be noticed—and it *will* close the doors to many job opportunities.

The positive habits you build into your life will make a big difference over time. Likewise, the negative habits you choose will have the opposite effect. It is a simple choice, but simple is not always easy. The choice is yours. Many people today, young and old, are making poor choices and developing bad habits. But that only makes your good habits shine all the brighter! As you identify the areas you need to improve and focus your efforts, you will separate yourself from the herd. If you stick with it, your efforts are sure to be noticed.

OVERCOMING FEAR

What's your greatest fear? For most people, it is speaking in front of a group—and ironically, public speaking is also a requirement for almost any desirable job. If you are skilled at anything, you will probably be asked at some point to stand up and explain it to others. For some, this fear is so overwhelming it keeps them from achieving the personal and professional success they deserve. If this is your problem, there are practical ways to overcome this fear and get on with your life.

Robert was one of my very best friends, and very smart, particularly in the area of math. Robert was the first and only one in his large family to graduate from college. He worked at a steel mill to pay his way through school and received a bachelor's degree in engineering. He was extremely creative; he was granted 17 U.S. patents for various inventions.

But Robert had one major problem: he was terrified by the mere thought of speaking in front of people—any people. He knew he had to find a way to overcome this fear if he was to reach the level of career success he expected of himself. He knew his fear was irrational, of course; he had all the skill and knowledge he needed to speak on any area of engineering. But this irrational, illogical fear was keeping him from achieving his goals, so he needed to find a way to overcome it and move forward.

A friend who was a teacher asked Robert if he would talk to a group of senior high school students who were interested in engineering as a career. Robert agreed because he knew he had to overcome his fear of speaking. He arrived at the school an hour early and sat outside on a bench nearly frozen with fear. But when he saw his friend, he got up, in spite of the fear, and gave the talk. He said it wasn't the best talk he ever gave, but he never again had that debilitating fear of speaking to a group.

I did not have a great fear of speaking in front of people because of my sixth grade teacher, Mr. White. God bless Mr. White. Every Friday afternoon, he asked us to stand up in front of the class and read a "story" we had created using the spelling words from that week's lessons. We were allowed to make the tale as silly as we wanted, as long as it did not say anything negative about a student or teacher. We competed for laughs and could hardly wait to read our brilliant lines of juvenile humor. Eventually even the shyest members of the class couldn't resist joining in. Everyone had fun. We didn't realize at the time, but Mr. White, the best teacher I would ever have, was teaching us creative writing as well as eliminating our fear of speaking in front of groups.

If you weren't fortunate enough to have a Mr. White as a grade school teacher, there are many ways you can work to eliminate your fear of speaking. Public speaking classes are available at many schools and colleges, and I encourage you to take one. You can also find, or create, opportunities to speak at clubs, organizations, or even at your church. It is easier to overcome this common fear when you are speaking to a group of friends or classmates.

I once had the pleasure of sitting next to Zig Ziglar during a seminar at which we were both speaking. Zig was the most highly sought-after motivational speaker of his time. He spoke to audiences as large as 60,000 people. I asked Zig, "Do you ever get completely over the fear of getting up to speak in front of an audience?"

"Oh no," he replied. "I am always nervous when I walk up to the stage. You never completely get rid of that and you wouldn't want to. It's what keeps you focused for the event. Once I start into my talk I settle down and I'm not so nervous."

You may not be afraid of public speaking; your fear may lie in some other area. If it is a roadblock to your success, you need to overcome that fear. Think of it in a positive way—if you didn't have fears, you could never develop courage. (If you have several fears, think how courageous you can become!)

Courage only comes from overcoming fear. If you have overcome your *biggest* fear, what is there left in life to be afraid of? One of the best books I have read on this subject is *How To Win Over Worry* by John Haggai[60]. If you have a fear to overcome (as most of us do), read this book.

Remember, we are speaking of debilitating and irrational fears. Not all fears are debilitating or irrational; for example, it is wise to retain your fear of punching a lion in the nose! Some fears are based in wisdom, rationality, and experience—keep those.

RULE TWO: SET GOALS

Write down your life goals and concentrate on achieving them

I s it wrong to have a goal of getting out and staying out of poverty? Is it wrong to organize your time and focus your talents on making money? Well, no—but watch out!

You have probably heard people say, "Money is the root of all evil," thinking they are quoting the Bible. But what the Bible *really* says is, "The *love of* money is at the root of all kinds of evil" (1 Timothy 6:10, emphasis added). The point here is that any good thing we seek in life can become a bad thing if we allow it to take *all* our attention and focus, if we allow it to rule our heart and be the love of our life. A good and abundant life requires balance.

Fortunately, there is a way to insure this balance in your life—*and it's fun!* It is the simple process of writing down your goals. That is what the world famous explorer and adventurer, John Goddard, did.

When he was fifteen years old, John Goddard was suddenly motivated to do something very unusual. He had been listening to a gathering of his relatives as they sat around the dining room table after Sunday dinner. Years later, he recalled, "All the adults I knew seemed to complain, 'Oh, if only I'd done this or that when I was younger.' They had let life slip by them. I was sure that if I planned for it, I could have a life of excitement and fun and knowledge."[61]

87

Most fifteen-year-olds would have discounted that conversation around the dinner table as the normal complaints of parents, or worse yet, accepted disappointments and regrets as an inevitable fact of life. But not John Goddard. John grabbed a yellow writing pad and took it to his room. *In about an hour*, he wrote down a remarkable list of everything he wanted to accomplish in his life. When he finished, he had listed 127 goals. That original list appears in the back of this book with a check mark next to each goal he completed (see Appendix B).

It is an extraordinary list for a fifteen-year-old to write, and what is most impressive is that it is not just a collection of childish wishes, but a thoughtful list of remarkably broad and difficult goals. Some of the things he listed had never been done before, such as kayaking the Nile and exploring the entire length of the Congo River.

But the list wasn't only about adventure and travel. Many of the things he wanted to achieve required learning, such as: "become an Eagle Scout, land and take off from an aircraft carrier, learn French, Spanish, and Arabic, read the works of Shakespeare, Poe, Hemingway (and fifteen other great authors), and play 'Clair de Lune' on the piano." It was an impressive list of goals for anyone—and astonishingly broad, thoughtful, and mature for a fifteen-year-old.

There are *three key facts* that made Goddard's list amazing. *First*, he didn't try to figure out *how* he would accomplish each item, or how he intended to finance his adventures or support himself. He was, after all, just fifteen and had not chosen a career, but regardless of the reason, young Goddard had remarkable insight by not trying to list how each item would be accomplished.

Trying to figure out the *how* of a goal only complicates your thinking and limits your creativity. Listing *what* you want to do is exciting—really exciting. Figuring out how it's all going to happen can get tedious and discouraging. The great thing about goals is that you don't have to work out the details up front. Setting goals is not about *how* but about *what* you want your life to be.

> ## IF YOUR GOAL IS EXCITING ENOUGH,
> ## THE "HOW" WILL APPEAR.

You have already read my story of choosing just *one goal*: making straight As in high school. Achieving that one goal was so powerful that it changed my entire life. It became my solid foundation from which all of the other exciting experiences could be launched. As soon as I decided on that one goal, I knew how powerful and life changing it would be. I had no idea, at the time, how to accomplish it; if I had tried to figure that out first, it would have seemed impossible—just another daydream. But it was so exciting, so fantastic to me, I just had a feeling I could find a way to do it. Because it was so exciting, I knew I had to try.

Some of the "hows" I came up with to achieve my goal in high school really weren't effective; wearing khakis to class probably didn't change any grades, and I probably could have gotten an A in health without playing football. But starting to read that summer did help; and my devotion to rigorous study did work. And so did answering every question asked in class. The goal was so exciting that I was willing to do *anything and everything* to achieve it. It is that attitude—that willingness—which makes the *how* appear once you commit to the goal. **Not everything you try will succeed, but everything you don't try is sure to fail.**

The *second key fact* about John Goddard's list is that it is *his* list, and no one else's. After listening to adults moaning and complaining, Goddard just picked up a yellow pad, went to his room and wrote down his life's goals. He didn't tell anyone; he didn't ask for permission or advice. He just did it. And you can, too.

> ## A GOAL MUST BE YOURS, AND YOURS
> ## ALONE, IF IT IS TO BE EXCITING.

Goals are only exciting when they are your own. They cannot be based on what your family, friends, teachers, or employers expect of you, or what they think would fit you. If you let others define your goals, you will be under their control the rest of your life. Your goal setting will not be exciting; it will become drudgery, and you will never achieve the rich and abundant life. Letting others choose your goals drains the fun out of living.

You can certainly include others in *achieving* your goals, however. Helping you achieve your goals may even become one of *their* goals. Since most people don't have life goals of their own, you will find that your excitement in working toward your goals becomes contagious, attracting other people to help you achieve what you want to do.

The *third key fact* about Goddard's list is that he wrote it down, and he did it quickly. Lots of people daydream about what they would like to do; you hear them talk about it all the time, usually with the words, "When I . . ."—when I grow up, when I finish school, when I get a better job, when the kids grow up, when I get some money, when I have the time, etc. As soon as you hear those words, you know it is just a passing thought, not something they are really committed to accomplishing.

Writing down your goals changes all that. Almost like magic, your goals move from talk to action—writing them down is your first action, and action moves goals to accomplishments. It causes you to think, and gives you a written record of your thoughts. It becomes a solid foundation you can use to check on your progress, and even to change, modify, add, or delete goals. It is one of the most powerful steps you can take to change and improve your life.

Why don't more people do this? There are many reasons. I didn't write down my goal of making straight As in high school, for instance. It was only one goal, so I didn't need to write it down to remember it; besides, it was such a huge and all-consuming goal that I didn't want any other goal competing with it. (The fact is, I never thought about making a big list of goals at that time; I would have felt buried by a big list of goals like John Goddard's.)

AN EASY WAY TO WRITE DOWN LIFE GOALS

During our early years in business, my brother and I worked at developing a new customer-centered approach to industrial tool manufacturing. We set up a nationwide chain of service locations which allowed us to provide the fastest and highest-quality customer service in America. We often talked about how to improve our organizational abilities. One day my brother gave me an interesting article on setting goals to organize your time for maximum benefit. As I read it, my thoughts went back to John Goddard and his 127 goals.

I decided to sit down and, for the first time in my life, write out a broad list of my life goals. I read Goddard's list once more and read several articles about how to write business and personal goals. Then I wrote out a list for myself under several broad topics, such as "Business Goals" and "Family Goals."

Like Goddard, I focused on *what* I wanted to accomplish, not *how* I would accomplish it. It became exciting to think of the possibilities, just like it had been with my successful one-goal strategy in high school. I thought, "Why haven't I done this before? I know it works because of my previous success." Regardless of the delay, I now had a great new list of goals to work toward.

This was just as powerful, just as life changing, and just as exciting as when I set out on my one-goal challenge. My effectiveness at work dramatically increased. I actually found that I had much more time with family and friends. But the most amazing effect was financial. The first time I wrote down my financial goals I thought they were actually out of reach. I was surprised to find that I had to increase my financial goals each of the next five years when I updated my goals list. Wow, it was like magic!

A few years later, I had the opportunity to join a group called Young Presidents Organization (YPO). The members of this group are all Presidents/CEOs of medium-sized companies. It provided a great opportunity to exchange ideas and experiences with other top business men and women. After talking to some of the YPO members about the system I had developed for writing my own life goals, a group of them asked me if I would be willing to show them how I did it. Having learned so much from others in the organization, I was glad to have an opportunity to respond.

This experience inspired me to develop a course on how to quickly write effective life goals. Over the years I have had the opportunity to give this class to many groups and individuals. Very few people have written life goals. Even highly successful individuals rarely have them. Most successful people have a financial plan, and some have a "bucket list" of adventures they would like to experience, but very few people create a more complete list of goals that covers all of the important aspects of their lives.

I wanted to know why, so I started asking people who came to the classes, and designed my method to address these excuses. Here are the most common reasons people gave for not writing down their life goals:

1. **I don't have enough time**: My method takes only a few minutes.
2. **I want to keep my options open, to be flexible and spontaneous**: Nothing about writing goals keeps you from moving to better options. That's why pencils have erasers and computers have delete keys. Only God writes in stone.
3. **I don't plan because I don't know what is going to happen in the future**: That is another way of saying, "I don't want to take control of my life, so I'm leaving it to others."
4. **If I write down my goals and don't accomplish them, I will feel like a failure**: This may be the most common reason people don't write down their goals. Once you write them down (your first action step) you must continue acting to achieve them. Achieving the first and simplest goals normally eliminates this fear, and the powerful excitement of personal growth takes over.

The most amazing reason ever expressed in one of my classes for not having established written goals is, "I'm afraid I won't set my goals big enough to be exciting, and small enough to be achievable." Wow! My method is dynamite for this because you only have to do the first part, which is to make your goal exciting. You don't have to think about how you will achieve them, because the excitement will create that for you. It is almost as if opportunities to achieve your goals begin to appear out of nowhere, like magic. (There is a reason behind the magic, which I will explain later.)

What if you set a goal so high that you don't achieve it? You will still be better, wiser, and more experienced for having tried, and who is to say you won't reach your goal in the future?

John Goddard's goals included several things that had never been done before, by anyone. He achieved some of his goals many years after he wrote his list. One of his original goals, written in *1940*, was to travel to the moon. It's OK to think big—in fact it's required. *Do it. Go for the moon.*

Now is your chance to take the first action step. You will need a lined tablet, a pen, and a clock to time yourself. Do Exercise One— and please don't jump ahead to read the next exercise! There is a good reason for this, and we will get there quickly.

It's time to *dream* and *think* BIG—you are not *required* to do what you write down; you can always cross it off the list later. You are completely in charge here. Don't worry about spelling and neatness. Write fast and furiously. Put down as many things as you can, and be broad, including family, career, social, spiritual, physical fitness, etc. And be honest. It's your life—what do you really want it to be? Do Exercise One now, without reading ahead.

LIFE GOALS: EXERCISE ONE

For *ten minutes*, write down everything you would like to do, all that you want to accomplish, during the rest of your life.
Stop at the end of ten minutes.

Stop right there!

> **Don't go on reading until you have done Exercise One. It will only take a couple of minutes. I promise you it will be worth it.**

LIFE GOALS: EXERCISE TWO

If you knew that you would be struck dead by lightning six months from today, how would you spend your last six months of life?

Take no more than *four minutes* to write down what you would want to do with that time.

(Assume everything related to your death has been attended to, i.e., Last Will and Testament, cemetery plot, etc.)

In my experience, there is usually quite a difference between the items people list in Exercise One and Exercise Two, because of the sudden time limitation. We tend to think we have all the time in the world, but of course, we don't. For most people, the life goals from Exercise One tend to focus on self—all the fun and exciting things *we* want to do. The list from Exercise Two tends to focus more on relationships—family and friends. The difference between the two lists is probably telling you that you need to move family/friends (relationships) to a higher priority when you combine the two lists into one (which we will do shortly). None of us can afford to miss out on these important relationships. For all of us, time is limited.

The first time I did this exercise myself, I wrote, "Let my parents know how much I love them" on my *second* (four -minute) list. I didn't have that on my first list. My relationship with my parents had not been good for many years. I left home at age sixteen and had spent little time with them since then. Even though there were some rough feelings between us, I knew that there was love and caring underlying these problems, and I realized it wasn't going to change unless I made the first effort to change it.

This was such an important item that I made it my first priority and traveled to see them a few weeks later. I told them I wanted five minutes to tell them how much I loved them and appreciated all the sacrifices they had made for me. They were speechless. I got my five minutes, and then we talked for several hours. Things didn't change immediately, but the change started that night. Over time, it dramatically improved my relationship with both of them, and that change lasted for the rest of their lives. This is only one example of how powerful writing life goals, and taking action to achieve them, can be.

Now it is time to pull *your* two lists into one and clean them up a bit. I have found it helpful to organize my life goals under major categories. If you do this it will probably make you think of something you forgot to include in your list. Remember, my Sunday school class didn't even think about health. If you think of something important that you have left out, now is the time to add it to your list.

Here are the major categories I use:

1. Health
2. Personal Relationships
3. Spiritual Development
4. Community Work
5. Location (where do you want to live & work)
6. Work (what do you want to do)
7. Leisure
8. Financial Plan
9. Odds & Ends

Two examples of life goals using this system are included in the back of this book (see Appendix C). The first is for a young person whose education is not yet completed. The second is for a young adult already starting a career and family. These examples are included only as guides, which you can use to create your own list. Exercise Three shows you how you can do this so that your list is easier to use and update.

LIFE GOALS: EXERCISE THREE

COMBINE THE TWO LISTS INTO ONE.

1) <u>DEFINE</u> your goals as clearly as possible under

2) Major Group Headings, and

3) <u>TYPE</u> them neatly, when you have them worded adequately (not worded perfectly). Use a computer for this if you can.

4) ON THREE PAGES OR LESS

5) <u>WITHIN</u> <u>THREE</u> <u>DAYS</u> – if you don't take your hand-written list and type it within three days, throw the list away; it isn't important to you. Life goals must be exciting, and if they aren't exciting enough to get you to do this last step, they are more likely to become a burden. This only works if you get excited about your goals and commit to accomplishing them.

6) <u>REVIEW</u> <u>GOALS</u> <u>REGULARLY</u> – a minimum of once each month. Keep your list where you can easily read over it in your spare time.

7) <u>REVISE</u> AND <u>UPDATE</u> – at least once each year. These aren't written in stone. Your life goals will change, as they should. If you revise them, retype the list completely. Putting your goals on a computer is best, because it allows for easy revision (save your old lists for comparison over time).

You may not want to follow my system for writing out your goals. That is fine. The important thing is to get them written down in the form most helpful to *you*. There are many books on writing and achieving goals. I found most of them too cumbersome and time-consuming. Many advise you to read your goals first thing every morning and set a specific date as a deadline for achieving each goal. I tried this, but it drove me nuts.

For me, reviewing my goals once a month and revising them once a year worked. I am most interested in how much I get done on an annual basis. I also started rating my performance based on how well I believed I had done each year. I rated myself as achieving 100 percent in most areas but never could rate my performance at 100 percent in all areas for an entire year. That is probably best. It means I am constantly making progress, but I was keeping my goals set at a very high level, which required me to stretch and grow.

THE MAGIC OF WRITTEN LIFE GOALS

There is a reason behind the "magic" you experience when using written life goals. You will be amazed at how often things "just seem to fall into place" once you have defined your goals. This happens because the process naturally orders and prioritizes the things that are most important to you. And, perhaps more importantly, it helps you eliminate things that aren't important to you. Limiting your objectives brings focus to your life and dramatically concentrates your power. Suddenly you will have a clear understanding of what to pursue and what to avoid on a daily basis. When you start to connect specific opportunities to your goals, it becomes much easier to see the important opportunities in front of you, and much easier to avoid the distractions you don't want in your life. This will help to keep you from getting side-tracked.

Knowing that you are advancing your life based on your written goals will give you a new confidence. You will know that your success is not an accident, but the result of your choices and your actions. These achievements lead to a new security—a more solid foundation. When you begin to feel this new confidence and security, you will be more inspired to seek new challenges and adventures. This cycle can take you as far as you want to go. It's like magic!

SHARING LIFE GOALS WITH OTHERS—CAUTION

Be careful here. You don't owe anyone an explanation. This is your life; these are your life goals; they must be exciting to you. If they aren't exciting to you, you won't reach them. Most people feel very vulnerable laying out their life goals in front of others. Life goals are areas deeply important to *you*—not others. Even unintentional criticism can be harmful here.

My general rule is, "Don't share your life goals with anyone who is not willing to share their personal written goals with you." When I teach classes on how to write life goals, I never ask anyone to share their list of goals. The one exception is that I encourage married couples to both complete written life goals and discuss them with each other. Even here you must be careful not to be critical. It is OK if spouses have some different life goals—these usually result in expanding the relationship into new areas to be enjoyed together. Don't be discouraged if your spouse is not as enthusiastic about life goals as you are. There are seasons to life. Your spouse may not feel as great a need for written life goals at this moment in time.

When I completed my full written list of life goals, I did not share them with anyone but my wife for several years. Eventually, I had experienced the fantastic power of life goals and was very confident in recommending them to other people. Bill, a close friend of mine, asked me to help him develop his life goals. I had taught other people how to do this with great success, so I agreed, but he wanted us to share our life goals so we could work toward achieving them together. I was a little reluctant to do this; I was already succeeding with my life goals and didn't see how this would help. After some further thought, I decided that this might be a new and positive experience.

It turned out to be all that and more. Bill's list of life goals was totally different from mine. One major category he listed was an entire area of life about which I had no prior knowledge or understanding. In fact, it was the first thing on his list. Another life-changing experience was about to unfold for me, which we will discuss next.

RULE THREE: SEEK GOD

Seek a powerful and positive relationship with God

I was not raised in the church. In fact, I don't remember if there was even a Bible in our home when I was growing up. We probably had one on a shelf somewhere, but I don't remember seeing it. My parents were not members of a church, but they usually took us to a service somewhere on Christmas or Easter. Church wasn't a priority in our house, and it was pretty much the same for everyone we knew.

Then when I was about twelve, my parents joined a small church and started attending every Sunday. Naturally, I was expected to go along. I thought it was boring. They signed me up for a confirmation class with all the other kids my age. The classes were almost as boring as church on Sunday. All I can recall about it was having to memorize the books of the New Testament, in order, and reciting them in front of the congregation one Sunday. I passed the test. They gave me a certificate of membership and a box of green envelopes for donations, and I was "in"—a certified Christian and a member of the church.

One Sunday morning they held a congregational meeting right after the service. One group got up and wanted to fire the minister; another group got up and opposed it. They had a big shouting match right there in the church. My parents didn't participate in the verbal brawl, but I was amazed that this took place in a church. At least it wasn't so boring that week.

The minister did get fired, and my parents left that church. They eventually joined another church, but by then I was older and they stopped insisting that I attend. Church held no interest for me and some of the people seemed hypocritical. I had no intention of ever participating in a church again.

I went through college and the Army, and then started in business without any religious involvement. The early years in business were a tough struggle, but my brother and I persisted, and we began to succeed. I was dating a fantastic young lady and after a few years we got married. We had two children, both boys, over the next three years. The business was doing well, I had a good family life, and yet there was something missing—something I couldn't define. Maybe having children got me thinking about it.

After I helped my friend Bill develop his life goals, we agreed to share our lists of goals and work on achieving them together. We exchanged our lists and read them.

I was not prepared for what I saw on Bill's list. At the very top he had written, "Understand and master the spiritual principles of Jesus Christ." I had no idea how I could help him with that. I didn't even understand what he meant. Bill was, and is, a practical business entrepreneur and a well-known business consultant. He didn't talk like a "Bible-thumping" Christian. I knew he and his family went to church, but I had no idea that he had such strong feelings about faith.

I was able to help Bill in some areas of business and financial planning, and in turn, he tried to explain how his Christian faith helped him in his business and family life. He never talked about a particular religion; he just talked about principles of life that Jesus described in the Bible, which Bill said he tried to apply to life and business. He studied the Bible and said it provided strong guidance and purpose in his life.

I was pretty uncomfortable with this, but I thought, "Maybe he's got something here. Maybe this is the 'something' I can't define that seems to be missing from my life." I couldn't think of how to state this, so I just added two words—Spiritual Development—as a new major category of my written life goals. I wasn't even thinking of Christianity when I wrote those words. That's not much of a step of faith, but I guess it was enough because some very interesting things started to happen in my life.

About two months after I added those two words to my life goals, my brother dragged me to a business conference being held in downtown Atlanta to hear Zig Ziglar and a bunch of other motivational speakers. One of the speakers was a fellow named Charles "Tremendous" Jones. I had never heard of him before, but I later learned he was a nationally and internationally known speaker. He spoke for only about fifteen minutes, but he had some great jokes throughout his speech and since I had a speech coming up, I thought I'd buy the recordings he was selling and use the jokes in my own presentation.

At that time, I lived in Atlanta, but I was doing a lot of work at our Indiana plant. It was a 450-mile drive from Atlanta to Indiana, which gave me a lot of time to listen to the recordings I had purchased from Charlie Jones.

I got the jokes I needed for my business speech, but I got a whole lot more. One of the recordings turned out to be a speech Charlie gave to the Christian Businessmen's Committee (CBMC). In that speech he talked about the frustrations of running a business, balancing all of the needs of marriage, and raising a growing family while seeking a full and abundant life. Like Bill, he used Christian spiritual principles to balance these conflicting demands in his life, and like Bill, he never talked about "religion" or mentioned what church he belonged to. The speech was hilariously funny, but there was tremendous wisdom sandwiched between the jokes. In his talk, Charlie demolished every preconceived and misguided notion I had about Jesus Christ and Christianity. During the next six months, I listened to that three-hour talk forty or fifty times.

The first few times I listened to the recordings, I just laughed continuously and enjoyed all of the jokes. And, yes, I have to admit, that I did steal some of the jokes and use them in my business talks. But after I got the jokes, I kept being pulled back to listen, over and over again, to the wisdom. And there was a great deal of wisdom to be found there. Charlie had a different and broader view of life than I had ever known.

He had a habit of pointing out a Bible verse to people and then asking them what they thought it meant. Of course, I had no knowledge of the Bible at the time. One of the verses he read was Romans 3:10:

"None are righteous, no not one."

That sounded good to me. I certainly knew I wasn't "righteous," I just didn't know everybody else wasn't. The next verse he read was the first part of Romans 3:11:

"There are none that understandeth."

If this was really what the Bible said, I was beginning to think I might be in pretty good shape. I sure didn't "understandeth" and was relieved to hear that apparently no one else did, either. The very next thing he read, the second half of Romans 3:11, was really surprising to me:

"There are none that seeketh after God."

This didn't make any sense to me. If nobody seeks God, why would so many people believe in God, and go to church, and read the Bible? Charlie jumped to another book in the Bible for the answer. He turned to Ephesians 2:8–9, and read,

"For by grace are we saved through faith. It is not of your own doing; it is a gift of God, not because of works, lest any man should boast."

I had to listen to the recording quite a few times before I started to understand this. What this verse seemed to be saying was that "salvation"—forgiveness, acceptance, and a relationship with God—weren't something I got in exchange for something I did. It was a free, unearned and undeserved gift from God. All I had to do was accept it with an honest heart and an open mind.

I was surprised by this. I always thought you had to be good to get God's approval, and I knew that I had not always been good. These verses were saying that God's acceptance and love weren't something I got in return for something I had to do; they were saying it was a free gift, right up front.

I decided to check it out in a Bible. I had written down the verses and numbers but I had to ask my wife, Sara, how to look up the verses in the Bible. In case you are as unfamiliar with these things as I was, I have written out how to look up a Bible verse at the end of Appendix D in the back of this book. Once I figured out how to do this, I found that Charlie Jones had read the verses just as they were printed. I found many other interesting things in there, too.

I was trained as a lawyer and experienced in business, so I was still pretty skeptical. I didn't immediately become a Christian, but I did start to read about the Christian faith, as well as other religions. I wanted some sort of proof.

I tried to find a factual and historical basis for the Bible, and I found a great deal. For example, I found that the books of the Bible are, by far, the most accurate ancient texts. There are 643 copies of Homer's *Iliad*, and only ten copies of *Caesar's Chronicles*. Yet these two ancient texts are among the most highly regarded for accuracy and authenticity, although none of these copies were made within five hundred years of the originals. By comparison, there are thousands (some estimates as high as 24,000) of authenticated copies of New Testament texts, some existing copies made within forty to seventy years of the original events.[62]

Here is another example. The ancient Romans were known for their detailed records and skeptics pointed out that there was no record of a Roman ruler in Jerusalem named Pontius Pilate. How could there be no Roman record of the governor they sent to Jerusalem who conducted the trial of Jesus described in the Bible? But in June 1961, Dr. Antonio Frova, an Italian archeologist, excavated an ancient staircase buried for two thousand years, and uncovered a carved stone dedicating the building in the name of "Pontius Pilate, Prefect of Judea."[63] I read that there has never been a single archeological discovery that has contradicted historical descriptions in the New Testament.[64] But the Bible was not written for use as a history text; it was written to reveal religious faith.

In the end, I have to say I could not find proof. "Proof" is in fact a term most accurately applied in science. Scientific proof means that an experiment can be repeated to produce the same results. This is not possible with historical facts. The best we can do with history is search for evidence. We are left to engage our minds and review the evidence to form our understanding and belief.

To me, one of the most surprising and convincing pieces of evidence about Jesus Christ is the New Testament itself. We know that it is the most reliable and authentic ancient text we have. The stories described in those books, in my mind and in my experience, simply ring true. They have that eloquent grace and undeniable truth that captures our imagination. They do not sound like they were made up, because they do not flatter the people who wrote them or the characters they describe. They portray real people, in all their confusion, failure, fear, self-doubt, desire, and compassion. These are people from whom we learn a great deal, but they are not perfect people.

Jesus alone stands out as just what he said he was: the way to live, in freedom, truth and light. He gives all there is to give, up front. We respond, not out of fear, but out of gratitude. But don't just take my word for it, investigate it yourself by reading about Jesus' life in the Bible.

"BECOMING A CHRISTIAN ISN'T ABOUT ACCEPTING A NEW CREED;
IT ISN'T ABOUT TURNING OVER A NEW LEAF.
IT'S ABOUT ACCEPTING CHRIST'S SPIRIT."

Oswald Chambers

Thankfully, I did get a chance to meet Charlie Jones. One day, I noticed a telephone number for Tremendous Life Books on the cover of the recordings. I was a little reluctant to bother this famous speaker and author, but I wanted to thank him for opening this whole new area of knowledge to me. So I picked up the phone and dialed the number.

To my surprise, Charlie Jones answered the phone. I told him that I had heard him speak in Atlanta, had purchased some of his recorded talks, and had listened to them many times. My only purpose in making the call was to thank him for his talks and to tell him how meaningful they had been to me. When he learned that my wife and I had started attending a church to better understand what he was talking about, Charlie got very excited and was very encouraging. We made arrangements to meet a couple of months later at his business, Tremendous Life Books, in Mechanicsburg, Pennsylvania.

Charlie Jones was a larger-than-life character. Not only was he 6-foot-3 and 225 lbs., but he seemed to have only one speed: *fast!* He led me around his Mechanicsburg bookstore, pulling books off of the shelf every few minutes saying, "Here, read page 136; it's tremendous." I had a big cardboard box full of great books by the time I was ready to leave.

He took me to lunch at a local Christian Businessman's Committee meeting and introduced me to many of his friends. Afterward, we went back to the bookstore and had some time to talk. At one point I said, "Charlie, I've thought about joining a church, but aren't there a lot of hypocrites in these churches?" And I'll never forget his reply. He looked me right in the eye and said, "Yes, that's true. There are a lot of hypocrites in our churches. But don't let that bother you; go on and join anyway. One more won't hurt." I had to laugh at that. Charlie had a great gift for packaging hard truths in sweet humor.

Then he said, "Now God's been talking to us in these scriptures. Let's talk to him." Charlie bowed his head and said a simple prayer: "Lord, this is Charlie Jones. I'm just a sinner saved by your grace. I never deserved it, but I thank you for it. You're a great God. Now John Segal is here, and he'd like to talk with you, too."

He really put me on the spot, but Charlie had given such a simple prayer, I knew I could follow that. I bowed my head and said something like, "God, I don't understand what being a Christian is all about. I don't understand much about the Bible, but it seems to be filled with the kind of answers I need. And if Charlie Jones is a sinner, I've got to be twice the sinner he is. I ask you to come into my life. I take you at your word and I believe it's true. Please come into my life."

Afterward, I told Charlie that I didn't feel any different. He said, "Good. Don't go by your feelings. People who go by their feelings will get blown away by the first good wind of adversity. Your feelings will deceive you, but Christ never will. You've accepted Him into your heart and that's where He'll stay forever. He'll never leave you."

"Now," he went on, "if you are really going to learn about this you need to get a Sunday school class to teach."

"That's a great idea," I said. "I'll do that right after I read the Bible."

"No, don't do that!" Charlie gasped. "You'll never do it. Just go down to your church and tell them you want to teach a Sunday school class of youngsters, middle school or high school, and the Holy Spirit will teach you everything you need to know, just when you need to know it."

I didn't know the Holy Spirit, but figured that if Charlie recommended him, he must be good. So that's what I did. To my surprise, the minister at the church had a group available for me to teach right away. I learned the Bible while teaching those classes. I taught those classes for nineteen years, and it was the single best learning experience of my life. My wife taught Sunday school classes for the younger kids, too.

> ## THE BEST WAY TO LEARN A
> ## SUBJECT IS TO TEACH IT.

The young people I taught in the Sunday school classes never told me I did a good job teaching; they never said they liked the classes. But they did show up on Sunday, and some of them brought their friends—from other churches. It's not the students' job to encourage the teacher; it's the teacher's job to attract the students by providing positive, engaging lessons that make them think. That is exactly what Jesus did.

Charlie Jones became my spiritual mentor and a good friend. I found that he was one of the top motivational speakers in the world. He had written many books, one of which sold over two million copies. He had a personal library of over 10,000 books and was one of the most well-read people I have ever met. I was amazed to learn, many years later, that he had never graduated from high school. Charlie was from a poor family with six children. As the oldest, he had to go to work before he could graduate in order to help support the family.

Charlie Jones introduced me to many highly successful people who were also Christians. You would recognize the names of many of these high-level national leaders, authors, and athletes. What impressed me about meeting these people was not their fame or accomplishments, but how *ordinary* they were. When they were performing in front of a crowd they were highly skilled and tremendously impressive. But when I had a chance to meet them on a personal basis, I found that they were people just like you and me—quite average people who had found an ability or need to focus their efforts; and they held a strong understanding of their faith in Jesus Christ. It was a foundational part of their lives, and it was an important part of their strength.

When I was young, I thought that getting a good education, focusing on written goals, working hard, and always doing my best was what it would take to achieve a rich and abundant life. I was wrong. It does take all of those things, but it also requires an understanding of God. My study, learning, and faith in Jesus Christ brought a new balance, depth, and breadth to my life. It would not be possible for me to live a rich and abundant life without it.

We put our faith in things every day. We have faith that the sun will rise, that the brakes will work, that the grocery store will have food, that we will live through the day. Some put their faith in the stock market, some put their faith in gold. Jesus once said that if your faith was only the size of a mustard seed it could still be enough to move mountains (Mathew 17:20). It's *not* about how much faith you have. It's *all* about what you put your faith *in*. I have found that the faith I have placed in Jesus Christ has never failed me. My best evidence is that bringing Christ into my life changed who I am— very much for the better.

As much as I would like to be able to do it, as much as this section of the book may seem to be advocating it, I am not trying to tell you that you must believe in Jesus Christ. If life has taught me anything, it is that I do not have the power to do that. All I can tell you is that my study and belief in Jesus Christ have brought a bright fulfillment to my life beyond what I ever thought existed. That is my experience.

I do believe that if you are to achieve a rich and abundant life for yourself, you can't ignore Christ. Was He the greatest liar of all time? Was He insane? Or was He just who He said He was? Read Mathew, Mark, Luke, and John in the Bible, and decide for yourself. And then, make a decision about Him, one way or the other. This is the best advice that I can provide. I have focused on it myself for many years and have found no better way.

PART IV: RICH

KEEPING THE GOOD LIFE

HOW TO MAKE MONEY
AND HOW TO USE IT

A good friend of mine recommended that I not use the word "rich" in the title of this book. He pointed out that there are so few people who make it from poverty to "riches" that it would be holding out false hope. I greatly respect this friend's opinion, so I gave this a lot of thought. As you can see, the word "rich" remains in the title. There are two reasons for this:

First, I use the word "rich" as a relative term throughout this book, often joined with the word "abundant." If you are poor and make it to the middle class, believe me, you feel rich. When my family moved from a rented trailer into *our own* tiny four-room house, we felt rich by comparison. To achieve a rich and abundant life you cannot compare yourself to what others have. There will always be someone who has much more. You can only compare your condition now to your old life—the place from which you started. And there is absolutely nothing wrong with making money; even a great deal of money. This is America.

Second, we need to stop having such low expectations for Americans in poverty.[65] Poor people are not stupid or lazy, and most will respond to reasonable opportunities for improvement. I know many people who have moved from poor to middle class and beyond, to achieve a rich and abundant life. A few of their stories are included in this book. My story is one of them. My friend was right in pointing out that too few in poverty move to middle class and beyond—that is why I have written this book. More will make it out of poverty if they are helped to focus on how to do it, rather than just maintained *in* poverty and forgotten.

If you read the simple (but not easy) rules we have covered and put them into practice, I believe you will begin to see a solid improvement in your life. I think this because it has been my personal experience. Although this book isn't only about money, it is clear that being able to improve your financial condition is necessary if you are to stay out of poverty and live a rich and abundant life.

These rules made a dramatic difference in every aspect of my life, and one of the most dramatic improvements was in the area of money. Because I believe this will be your experience, I have included this section to provide you with further insights I have discovered, and to guide you to some of the tools you may find helpful to achieve increased prosperity. I strongly encourage you to look into the books and websites referred to in this book.

WEALTH ATTITUDE AND THE MARGIN OF SECURITY

The character of Ebenezer Scrooge, created by Charles Dickens, has had an enormous influence on our view of wealth. Dickens did a great job of capturing the essence of a person whose ultimate goal is the hoarding of money. Scrooge's twisted, miserly, penny-pinching, lonely, stingy, self-absorbed, bah-humbug addiction to the accumulation of gold became a classic. At the end of the story, he finds it is not too late to find joy through generosity and friendship.

I have always liked the Disney version of this character: Scrooge McDuck, the richest man (fowl?) in the world, who keeps all of his money in a "money bin" and uses a bulldozer to push it around for fun. When a chipmunk steals a quarter from the money bin, Scrooge, with the help of Huey, Dewey, and Louie, spends a fortune chasing the rodent all over the world to get back his quarter.

Men (and fowl) like this obviously have a problem with their focus. However, a surprisingly large number of Americans seem to accept the Scrooge character as the true personality of anyone who owns a business or develops a personal plan to really improve their financial condition.

This is a false, demeaning, and destructive characterization of people who save and invest.

The objective of every investment and business *must* be to make money. Creating a profit is necessary to survival for every business and every successful person. Even non-profits must create a "profit"—a surplus over and above their expenses—to survive; the only difference is non-profits don't pay taxes. The capitalist idea of making a profit is the only way wealth is created. This system allows for the improvement of living conditions for people throughout the world.

And yet I hear college students apologize for being business majors, quickly noting that they plan to work for a non-profit, or go to Africa to improve water systems. Those are noble goals, but they have it backwards. The more skilled you become at creating wealth, the better able you are to help other people improve their daily lives.

So I am amazed when I hear people refer to making money as an "evil" objective. There are two types of people who talk about money this way—those who don't have much money, and those who have a lot of money but feel guilty about how they got it. I never have to explain the need for profit to people who have really been poor; they understand the concept from personal experience.

I hope that this book makes it clear that money, in and of itself, is not a worthwhile goal. Money is not good or evil; it is simply a necessity of life. Air, water, and food are also necessities of life. Just as you would not want food and drink to become the single focus of your life, neither would you want money to be the single focus of your life. While real-life "Scrooges" are rare, the fictional character presents a warning worth noting. The value of having money isn't the money itself; it is what you can do with it to make your life and the lives of others better.

Getting to the level of personal wealth you want to achieve is half attitude and half knowledge. While it takes both, a special order is once again the important factor. You have to have the right attitude *first*. That's why most of this book has been about how you see and react to the world around you. You have to develop the right attitude first if you are to get the money you need to achieve your goals in life.

Many of the truly wealthy people I know do have very nice homes, furniture, clothes, cars, etc.; some even have airplanes. I also know some people who have all these things, but are up to their ears in debt and really can't afford to live that way. What's the difference? People who become truly wealthy are able to wait on purchasing things until they have the money to pay for them—without debt. That is a very big difference.

> THE ABILITY TO DELAY PERSONAL PLEASURE IS THE BIGGEST DIFFERENCE BETWEEN THE TRULY WEALTHY AND THEIR IN-DEBT LOOK-ALIKES.

Many very wealthy people don't flaunt their wealth at all. They live their lives pretty much the same way they lived before they became wealthy. In fact, most of the wealthy people I know live like this. They live well, they have all of the things they want and need, but they have no interest in showing off their wealth to impress other people. Many of them take care of individuals in need and give generously to charitable causes, but you will never hear about it from them. They are confident and secure about who they are. That is a good way to live.

People who live in abundance live well, having all the things they want and need. But to live well, they have set limits on themselves so that they never use up all of their resources for living.

Once again, this is a very simple concept. But it is not easy because these people have the same temptations to overspend as anyone else. However, they have mastered the ability to control those temptations in order to save and invest for their future. This is what I call *wealth attitude*, and it is the first and most important thing you must work to develop if you are to accumulate wealth.

> ## WEALTH ATTITUDE MEANS LIVING WELL
> ## BY LIVING <u>WELL BELOW</u> YOUR MEANS.

People do not develop a wealth attitude *after* they are wealthy; they develop it while they are getting wealthy. In the early years, they don't have the best of everything, but they make the best of everything they have. Their focus is not on impressing others, and not on all the meaningless stuff that money can buy.

They live well *below* their means—below the level at which they could live if they spent all they earned and more, by going into debt. Because they are living below their means, on less than their full income, they can save, invest, handle unexpected expenses, and gradually improve their standard of living—*without* debt. This positive gap between income and spending provides a critical *margin of security* which, over time, makes living easier and more enjoyable.

The margin of security consists of savings or assets which allow you to get through rough economic times—periods of financial loss. Success is not a straight line of progress; you will always experience good times and bad. The economy goes through ups and downs, and not every financial decision will be a winner. Every successful person learns to create and build their own safety net of value for economic security. You don't have to be rich to live like this, but it is more likely that you will get rich living like this.

These people do not borrow and spend to impress others. Instead, they focus on developing their margin of security. They do not compare themselves to others; they compare themselves to where they were when they started. This is the only valid comparison we can make regarding money.

Most millionaires in America live like this. They are all around you and you are probably not aware that they have wealth. Most of them are small business owners who continuously invest their margin of security back into their own businesses to keep them strong and growing. Since they provide most of the jobs in America, their success becomes their community's success. It is a positive cycle of expanding prosperity—for everyone.

THE MARSHMALLOW TEST

We are speaking, of course, of *delayed gratification*, which I mentioned earlier in this book. I told you how I first discovered this principle when I took charge of cleaning out the garage. What I didn't know at the time was how important this principle would be to my future success.

When I thought about it, though, I realized I had actually used this idea much earlier in my life. When I was eight, I had a lot of cavities and had to go under the dentist's drill. It was painful. The dentist noticed I had been chewing gum, a regular habit at the time, and told me it was bad for my teeth. So I decided, then and there, never to chew gum again—not to cut down, but to quit for good. And I did. It wasn't easy, because I liked gum and Mom always kept a pack in her purse. To overcome the temptation, I thought about the dentist's drill. I still can't think about gum without thinking about dentist drills.

But it wasn't only the thought of dentist drills which helped me keep my commitment to stay away from gum. It gave me a feeling of personal strength and control to turn down gum when it was offered. Everyone always took gum when someone offered it—everyone but me. Exercising my own self-will became a reward in itself.

I don't know if quitting that habit eliminated my cavities—fluoride in the water probably did that—but I liked the fact that I made the decision myself, and never gave in to the temptation. You may think that was unimportant, but it is the same stubborn, "I'm going to do this" attitude I needed to clean up the garage, and later to change my performance in school.

This same attitude helped me quit smoking in high school. When the first Surgeon General's report came out linking smoking to cancer, I decided never to smoke another cigarette, and I stopped. Later in life I learned that this principle of taking charge and making a decision in order to achieve a better future—*delayed gratification*—had been found to be highly important in a famous psychological experiment called "The Marshmallow Test."[66]

In the 1960s, psychologist Walter Mischel conducted a series of experiments on impulse control at Stanford University. His test was very simple: pre-school children were given a choice of one marshmallow right now, or *two* marshmallows if they waited alone in a room, with nothing to do, until the "teacher" returned. The marshmallows were right in front of the children and all they had to do was push a buzzer, the teacher would immediately return, and they could eat the one marshmallow—or they could wait until the teacher returned on his own, without the buzzer, and get the greater reward of eating two marshmallows.

The researchers then followed the lives of those tested, with surprising results. It turned out that the children who were able to delay gratification and wait for the second and greater reward of two marshmallows were more successful in various areas of life—school, career, even their health. Impulse control or delayed gratification— the ability to see and wait for a bigger reward in the future—has been proven to be a key factor in achieving long-term goals. It is certainly a key factor in achieving a rich and abundant life.

Another important finding of these experiments was the discovery that impulse control is an ability that can be developed. Some people are better at this early in life, but all of us can improve this important ability to act in a particular way now, in order to get a better result in the future. It is not something you either have at birth or don't have—it can be learned and improved with practice.

You can immediately see how developing this ability could help your wealth attitude. Delaying spending impulses helps to build your financial margin of security. If you want to achieve a rich and abundant life, you must develop this ability. Setting goals and working to achieve them—at any age—is a great way to develop this critical skill. But delayed gratification is only part of the equation.

THE "GRIT" FACTOR

In 2010 I met four-time Olympian Rubén González. We became friends while climbing Mt. Kilimanjaro. At Uhuru Peak, its ice-covered summit, Kilimanjaro reaches the height of 19,340 feet, making it the highest mountain on the African continent. During the climb and the week-long photo safari that followed, I had a chance to hear about Rubén's life. It is a fascinating story.

At the age of ten, Rubén watched the Olympics on TV and began to dream of becoming an Olympic athlete. Although he played soccer in college, he was not considered a gifted athlete. But this did not stop him from pursuing his dream.

"My strength wasn't athletic ability. My strength was perseverance and tenacity. I wasn't a quitter. I was a bulldog. The challenge was to find an Olympic sport so tough, a sport so dangerous, a sport that resulted in so many broken bones, that there would be a lot of quitters. Let everyone else quit. That way, maybe I could rise to the top through the attrition rate."

The Olympic sport Rubén chose was luge. This involves piloting a four-foot-long, flat fiberglass sled with two steel runners at speeds of up to ninety miles per hour down an ice-covered, curving, half-pipe track. There are no brakes. The rider steers, using subtle shoulder movements through multiple turns, pulling up to six Gs in the curves (jet pilots are trained not to exceed five Gs in combat). His chosen sport did result in multiple broken bones. There is much more to Rubén's fantastic life story, which you can read about in his autobiography, *The Courage to Succeed*.[67]

Why would anyone do this? Delayed gratification is certainly required for the years of training and supporting oneself financially through four consecutive Winter Olympics. But there is another element to such achievement, which I did not fully understand. It's called "grit." Rubén González is the "grittiest" person I have ever met. Psychologist Angela Duckworth has described this personal trait in great depth in her best-selling book, *GRIT: The Power of Passion and Perseverance*.[68]

Through her own research and multiple studies Angela Duckworth shows that *passion* and *perseverance*, over which we have great control, are powerful factors for determining what each of us achieves in life. While passion and perseverance are available to everyone, they are most effective for those who are willing to take charge of, and responsibility for, their own achievements in life.

When you TAKE responsibility, it GIVES you control.

CONTROLLING THE FLOW OF YOUR MONEY

If you are ever to get ahead financially in life, you have to know how much money you are making and how you are spending it. You do this by writing down your monthly income and then listing each monthly expense below it. This is called a budget, and it's your most basic financial tool.

You have to know how much money you are making every month and how much you are spending before you can begin to get control of your money. It's pretty easy to see what you are making each month, but you are going to be surprised to see how much you are spending and where you are spending it once you write it all down. You will need to get control of your spending first. *You can do this.*

For some people, budgeting is a logical and simple practice. Others resist it like poison. I am not a psychologist so I can't say what causes these differences in personalities. I think some people are frightened by numbers or think that "finance" is difficult, complicated, and confusing. If you fall into this group, I have nothing else to tell you but that you have to overcome your own resistance. And you can, because it is not difficult, complicated, or confusing—in fact, the whole key is to keep it very simple.

HELP FROM DAVE RAMSEY

Fortunately, the process of setting up a personal budget has been made incredibly easy thanks to Dave Ramsey, a man who went through tremendous difficulties with money. He even went bankrupt when he was young, but he didn't give up. He made it his goal to learn how to earn and save money, and he overcame his financial problems. In fact, he got so good at overcoming money problems that he decided to share his ideas with others. You have probably heard him on his daily radio program, *The Dave Ramsey Show*, where he gives great advice to people who are struggling to change their financial lives.

Recently, Dave Ramsey spent a year of his time and millions of dollars developing a very simple and effective way to set up a budget. To top it off, he made it available to everyone, online, free of charge. This is a man who lives a rich and abundant life and is working to make that dream come true for others. To use Dave Ramsey's free online budgeting tool, go to:

https://www.daveramsey.com/tools/budget-forms/

When you get to the site just start filling in the blanks. It's that simple. If you don't have a computer, go to the public library and use theirs.

The best and easiest way to set up your budget is on a computer. You'll need basic computer skills to achieve your goals, so you may as well get skilled enough right now on a spreadsheet program. Computer knowledge will make your financial planning—and your life— much easier.

You can get a lot more help from Dave Ramsey. I have listed some of his books and courses in Appendix D. His book, *The Total Money Makeover*, is an easy-to-read classic on how to improve your financial life. Dave has a great personal story. He understands what it is to be broke and to work your way up to a rich and abundant life.

Many local churches teach his course, Financial Peace University, and I strongly recommend it. Married couples will want to take the course together to make their efforts twice as powerful. The Ramsey organization also has a program for high schools, home schools and colleges (see Foundations® in Personal Finance).

WHAT IS WEALTH?

If you had a million dollars in cash, would you be wealthy? Is wealth a big pile of cash? If so, how much? Have you thought about that? The problem with thinking of wealth as a big pile of cash, like Scrooge McDuck and his money bin, is that it doesn't consider the important factor of *time*.

If you had a million dollars in cash and you were going to live for fifty more years, you would have only $20,000 per year to live on (we'll forget about investing and earning interest for the moment). That $20,000 per year is well below the poverty line for a family of four. When considering money, *time* makes all the difference.

People who are actually creating wealth don't see it as a pile of money. They see it as value to be invested in different types of assets which will give them a profit—a return on their investment. They look at money like a farmer looks at seeds. The farmer doesn't hoard his seeds in the barn—he plants them to grow a crop he can sell, buys more seeds, and keeps the extra money as profit. Profits are what we *all* live on. To create wealth you have to grow your money by investing it in your own business or other investments; it is "seed money."

Here is a useful definition of wealth:

> ### *"WEALTH IS A PERSON'S ABILITY TO SURVIVE SO MANY DAYS FORWARD."*[69]
> *R. Buckminster Fuller*

What Fuller means is that if you are living on $10 dollars a day and you have $100 dollars, you are "wealthy" enough to "survive" for the next 10 days. If you want to live ten times better (in financial terms), you'll need $100 per day, or $1,000 to survive for the next ten days.

This, of course, begins to get you thinking about what happens at the end of ten days, when the money runs out. Good thinking! You need a way to get more money. Hopefully, you can figure out a way to have a continuing flow of cash for your future—like a *job*, maybe?

Thinking of money as a means to adjust your standard of living allows you to see money as a tool for growth rather than a final objective. If your lifestyle requires $1000 a week you will need to have a job which pays $52,000 per year ($1000 per week for fifty-two weeks). If you want to improve your lifestyle to a level of $2,000 per week you will need a job which pays $104,000 per year. If you save and invest, your objective is then to have your income producing investments (your small business, stocks, rental properties, etc.) generate $2000 per week in income. Once you do this, you no longer need the income from your job. When you have accomplished this, you have become "independently wealthy" because your investment income is enough to pay for your lifestyle.

This is what creating wealth is all about: developing a plan to continue a flow of money that supports your standard of living now and into the future. If you want to raise your standard of living, you have to develop a plan to increase the amount of money you will be receiving in the future.

Most Americans do not have any desire to amass a great fortune.[70] They just want to be able to save enough money to live an abundant, secure life.[71] For you, this may be enough money to quit working and retire, to educate your children, to travel, to live where you want, or to contribute generously to the charities you love. You can do these things. You can figure out how to become financially independent using some of the ideas in this book, along with your own brains and determination.

HOW MOST AMERICANS DEVELOP WEALTH

Over 80 percent of American millionaires are "first generation rich"— they did not inherit any wealth.[72] They had to figure out a way to earn it. Of course, we all have to figure out a way to earn a living, but the big difference is that we don't all use the money we earn in the same way.

Most wealthy Americans start with a job of some kind, just like everyone else, but the similarities stop there. The average person's paycheck goes first to pay the *minimum* amount possible on their mortgage, car loan, credit card payment, student loan, etc., and whatever is left over is "fun money." If they get a raise at work, they keep paying the minimum on their loans and increase the "fun money."

They view a raise as a chance to improve their lifestyle; they see it as "extra" money to be spent on enjoying life. They spend it on cars, homes, boats, clothes, gifts, parties, eating out, vacations, and all kinds of other fun stuff. When the income they make isn't enough to cover all of the fun stuff, they borrow money. The average new car *loan* is now more than $30,000 over a term of sixty-eight months—unbelievable.[73]

> ## DEBT
> ## ENJOYING THE PLEASURE NOW
> ## AND PUSHING OFF THE PAIN
> ## UNTIL . . . DISASTER.

The easiest, most common, *and most expensive* way to borrow money is to get a credit card and only pay the minimum amount each month. The average interest rate on credit card debt is 15 percent, and the average American with credit cards has more than $16,000 in credit card debt.[74] Others get in debt to the bank with student loans, car loans, or home equity loans. They may be hardworking professionals with high salaries, and very good at their jobs; they may *appear* to be very successful, but they are in financial trouble.

This is not how people who become wealthy live their lives. People who become wealthy may start out with the same job and the same income, but they *use* money differently. Instead of using their income to maximize their "fun" they use it *first* to decrease expenses, then to save, and finally to invest.

For example, they redirect the money that others spend on "fun stuff" toward paying off their car payment or student loans. With those debts paid off, they have fewer monthly payments, and suddenly they have more money available. But even then they don't use the increase in available funds for "fun." They use it to pay off the house mortgage and every other debt they may have. Once all the debts are paid off they start placing the extra money in income-producing investments—these investments become income producing *assets*.

123

This is what my friends who started small businesses have done. They saved and invested their profits in equipment and capital improvements. The growing list of equipment (assets) increases their ability to earn money by offering new services. The business itself is a growing asset, which provides them with continuous income. Most people who become financially secure in America start out with little or nothing and learn to use money in just this way.

It may appear to be easier to spend all you earn and borrow. Like drugs, it may even feel good at first. But as debts pile up, you have less and less "excess money" to spend. You are paying more and more interest on debts and eventually find that the credit cards are maxed out and no one will lend you more money.

The typical attitude of those in this situation is, "Hey, I work hard at my job and I'm good at it; I'm not a bum. Don't I deserve to have a little fun? Why should I put off gratification? I want to have fun while I'm still young enough to enjoy it. Life is too short. If I lose my job I'll collect unemployment for a while and catch up on the bills later. I can get another job. I'm doing OK. Don't tell me how to live my life."

Spenders and borrowers are really nothing more than employees of their creditors. They are trapped, focusing on the need for money just to keep their heads above water and keep up the false appearance of prosperity. It is sad, it is common, and it is unnecessary. You don't have to be that person. You don't have to live like this. Smart people save more of their money.[75]

HELPING OTHERS AS YOU GROW

Contrary to the Scrooge image, I have found that giving is a common thread among most business owners. Remember, Brad, Tom, Juanita, and Landy? They all give generously to the community in which they live—not only financial support, but also with their personal time. People who see needs in the community and fulfill them through the goods and services their businesses provide also tend to see other needs as well, and because they are people of action, they often use their skills to assist others.

If you are satisfied with your living standard you may decide you actually want to be able to *give* more—perhaps a great deal more—to others. If you aren't willing to decrease your living standard and you don't have a lot of unneeded cash lying around, you have to develop a way to generate more income in order to increase your giving to others. How's that for a positive slant on creating wealth?

I know several wealthy people who look at working and earning money in just that way. They have enough money to live a secure lifestyle even if they quit working. But they like the work they do, and they continue to work to increase their ability to help others in need. Being able to help others succeed is one of the greatest joys in life. And you don't have to be "wealthy" to do this.

There are many examples of Americans who have used great wealth to help others. Andrew Carnegie was a steel baron who made a vast fortune in the first half of his life; then he gave it all away building thousands of free public libraries throughout America to help others get an education through books. Bill Gates and Warren Buffett, modern-day billionaires, have put much of their money into charitable organizations to improve health and education worldwide. Dave Ramsey supports many charitable causes and encourages others to do so on his radio programs and in his books. Mark Zuckerberg, creator of Facebook, announced that he was giving most of his company stock to charities. Larry Page, cofounder of Google, gave $177 million to charities in one year. But you don't have to wait until you are wealthy to help others. You will find that helping others provides its own rewards.

COULD YOU START YOUR OWN BUSINESS?

When I asked my Sunday school students what they wanted to learn, their answers surprised me. For example, almost every year they asked for classes on how to make money. I created a series to meet this request, and their response to these lessons was very positive. The series encouraged many of my students to get involved in business or pursue professional careers.

One of my students became interested in learning how to invest. I gave him some basic books on investing and a board game which taught the principle of cash flow. This student went on to get a master's degree in business administration (MBA), specializing in finance. He works in the financial industry today. Some of my other students got business degrees in college and went on to get MBAs, including one of my sons.

Quite a few of my students have regular jobs but have started small real estate investment companies on the side. They rent houses to people and use the rental income to pay off the mortgages of the property. Several of them became plumbers, electricians, doctors, and dentists, and have purchased the buildings in which they work. Instead of paying rent to others, they are building assets which will appreciate in value over the years.

Two of my students, Evan and Drew, decided to start a car cleaning and detailing business during their sophomore year in high school. After school and during their summer vacations, they would clean cars. At first they were slow and weren't making much for their time and effort. But by focusing on the process, they were able to reduce costs and the time required for each car to less than half that of their competitors. They accomplished this while keeping their customers happy and growing their business. Both of them were able to save money from their profits for college.

Evan kept up the entrepreneurial spirit in college by starting a campus publication for fraternities and sororities during his senior year. He expanded the publication to all of the major universities during the next few years after graduation. In 2014, Evan's company launched an exciting new online publication focused on millennials, with the goal of giving real people a voice and democratizing the world's news and social content. It is one of the nation's fastest-growing businesses, and he recently raised $33 million to expand the business worldwide. Check it out for yourself at https://www.theodysseyonline.com/.

Starting your own business isn't the first thing you need to do. First you need to concentrate on making sure you understand and commit to using the rules described in the first part of this book. But at some point, I hope you will consider starting your own small business. It will teach you more than any other experience about the interaction of planning, teamwork, and money.

I have to warn you that most people who start their *first* business fail.[76] But even if your first business attempt fails, you will have learned a great deal from the experience. You will know more on your second try, and eventually you will succeed. This "Try-Fail-Try Again-Succeed" experience is very common among successful people, and is one of the reasons it is beneficial to start work experience early in life. It isn't any different than learning how to play a sport or a musical instrument. You don't quit because you don't do it well on the first try—you keep trying until you do it well.

Some people have dreams of starting a business, but never do it because they are afraid of *risk*; they think business people have to take big risks to succeed. My experience is that most successful businesses are not started by big risk takers; they are started by average people who have some business knowledge from their work experience and decide to start small in a field they already know.

> ## RISK COMES FROM NOT KNOWING WHAT YOU'RE DOING.
> Warren Buffett

They have some knowledge of what it takes to run a business and they spend a lot of time developing financial and business plans to reduce their risk. There is still risk, of course, but it's minimized by their planning and knowledge.

Many business owners start by purchasing a small business which already has a few knowledgeable employees, some operating equipment and a customer base so that they don't have to start from scratch. This is often possible when a small business owner wants to retire and looks for someone to buy them out. The selling owner may even be willing to mentor the buyer for a period of time. There are risks in owning any business, but also ways to minimize the risk.

The second reason I want you to consider starting your own business is because it is good for America. It is the entrepreneurial spirit, the can-do attitude, and the innovation of new ideas which has made our nation the envy of the world. Small businesses provide 54 percent of all sales and 55 percent of all jobs; more importantly, they account for 66 percent of all *new* jobs in America.[77] Small businesses give job opportunities and experience to young employees. A tremendous amount of innovation comes from small businesses because they need to innovate to survive. They don't have the money and staying power of big companies, so they have to respond quickly to customer needs.

I don't think the American public has much knowledge of, or appreciation for, the difficulty and importance of these entrepreneurial efforts. Most Americans seem to think that business owners make huge amounts of money that they spend on extravagant living standards.

Our local school system sends all the eighth grade classes to various businesses one day each year to learn about how to get a job and how businesses operate. It is a good program, so my company hosted a class each year. We always structured the classes to start with a question. We asked the students how much profit they thought three types of businesses—a manufacturer, a retail store, and grocery store—made *after* paying their expenses and taxes each year. They were asked to write down the percent of after-tax profit on a sheet of paper for each business, then we added up the numbers and compared the class average to the actual facts.

Here are the results (averaged over many years of classes).

What Is <u>After Tax</u> Profit of Businesses in America?		
Type of Business	Students' Guess	Actual Profit
1. Manufacturer	41%	6.0% [78]
2. Clothing Store	46%	3.4% [79]
3. Grocery Store	30%	1.5% [80]
Averages:	39%	3.6%

The first time we gave this unscientific survey, I couldn't believe the results. Did these bright young people really think that businesses made *that* much money—when the reality was so different? But these numbers were about the same for all the eighth grade classes over a period of at least ten years. If you are thinking that these are just uninformed middle school kids, I hate to tell you that you are wrong. A recent national poll asked this same question of American adults, and their average guess for the profitability of companies was 36.4 percent[81]—not much different from the responses of our eighth graders. Amazing!

I have included this because it indicates how little the general public knows about American business and how hard it is to actually run a business. I also include this to highlight how extremely tight the margins of profit are for most businesses in America. Owning your own small business is still the best way to create wealth in America, but if you choose this path, be ready for hard work, long hours, and employees who think you are already rich.

This also explains why most small business "millionaires" don't appear to be rich. Most of what they earn after taxes and expenses (that small percentage of after-tax profits) has to go back into the business to keep it going. Owning your own business can give you a great sense of security, but most business owners don't really have a lot of money until they sell their businesses and retire.

You have probably heard a lot about the "disparity of income" in our country—the 1% versus the 99%. The media regularly describes the 1% of highest wage earners as owning most of the country while the suffering 99% struggle to make a living on low wages paid by the greedy 1%. This is the Scrooge myth all over again. They make it sound like the top income earners are a group of controlling owners who manipulate everyone else. This is false.

The truth is that most of the people listed by the Internal Revenue Service as the top 1 percent of income earners each year do not earn that high amount year after year—in fact most of those high incomes are not from salaries at all, but business owners and investors who are "cashing out." More than 70 percent of the income earners on the IRS top list are only there for one year. They are people who have delayed "instant gratification" by reinvesting in their businesses for many years and are now selling those business assets to retire.[82]

Why should I even talk about the misconceptions of the American public regarding businesses and the pursuit of wealth? This is America where the struggle to get ahead has always been a part of our culture, and a goal of our people. This is what creates jobs for all of us. Young entrepreneurs create new business ideas that challenge and eventually replace old technology and outdated business structures. It is a cycle of constant renewal and rebirth. Yet there is a persistent and growing criticism of this proven system that discourages our young people from going into for-profit business as if "profit" is a dirty word. This is utter nonsense and it is destructive to the creation of jobs and wealth, which we desperately need to support all Americans.

So here is another "Scrooge Myth" for debunking: The top 10 percent of American households by net worth own 75 percent (about $60 trillion) of the total wealth of the country, while 90 percent of households hold the remaining 25 percent ($20 trillion). This is deceptive because of the numbers, which our government uses, and the numbers it ignores.

Our government requires and collects payroll deductions from working people for Social Security, Medicare, and Medicaid. These taxes greatly decrease what average working people can save and invest. However, these "wealth" comparisons don't count the *value* of future payments to our citizens who have been taxed for these programs.[83] If our government did count the value of these future payments to its citizens, that value would add an estimated $95 trillion to these lower and middle class incomes. The top 10 percent do own a large percentage of the nation's wealth because they have invested their money in *assets*. If our government would count what they owe back to our people in future payments from Medicare, Social Security and other retirement programs, the distribution of American wealth would be shown to be much more evenly distributed.

Here is another question we asked those eighth grade classes that visited our company each year:

Where does our government keep the Social Security Trust Fund?

1) Department of Labor, Washington, DC,

2) Fort Knox, Kentucky, or

3) A secret government location.

Sorry, it's a bit of a trick question. The payroll deduction taken out of your check every payday (6.2 percent from you plus 6.2 percent from your employer, or 12.4 percent total)[84] goes into the Federal government's general fund and is spent each year. There is no cash "fund" of invested money to support Social Security.

The Treasury Department does keep a record of what was paid into the "fund" and estimates what is "owed," as well as a calculated "interest" on the funds, but these are just accounting entries. There is no actual cash "fund." More like an IOU, it is all based on our federal government's promise to pay out of future taxes.[85] That is another reason you need to work to develop your own assets and savings for the future.

ACTION

Y ou can start using the information you have learned in this book at any age—in fact, the younger, the better. Your attitude and early experience makes all the difference.

Don't let those who are doing nothing tell you that you can't reach a better life. I am telling you, from my own experience that it can and is being done every day by many people. Taking action on these things is easier and less expensive while you are still young. **Work on getting a good education first**; it will give you the solid foundation for everything else you achieve.

It is the same thing with business experience. Get some basic business experience when you are young, whether it's mowing lawns, washing cars, working with computers, baking cakes, or a thousand other skills you can learn at any age. You don't have to be good at it on the first try—in fact, don't expect to be! We all learn from our mistakes. The important thing is not to get discouraged and quit. If you keep trying, eventually you will succeed. Start now. Do it while you are young. When you are older, learning from your mistakes in business is *much* more expensive. I know this from personal experience.

Through Charlie "Tremendous" Jones, I got to know many great nationally known speakers and writers. Several of them told me that very few people in their audiences (they estimated only 5–10 percent) ever take action to implement the new ideas they hear in a speech or read in a book. People get excited at first but it doesn't last very long: "Wow, what great ideas! I'm going to use them to change my life. I am so fired up. No one can stop me now. I'm going to start on this as soon as . . . right after . . ."

You already know the rest of this story. They get busy with their old routine and don't make any changes. A few months later, they find the notes they took from the motivational talk, or the book they read, and they put it in a drawer somewhere, thinking, "I'll get back to that a little later." Those notes will still be in the drawer for their relatives to throw out after the funeral.

But some people, the 5–10 percent, *take action right away*, and that makes all the difference. Think of John Goddard—what an exciting life he led! He refused to accept the attitude of his relatives, talking about all the opportunities they had missed. He took *action*—immediately—by quickly writing down what he was going to do, and then started taking *action* to achieve the things that were possible at his age. At age fifteen, he could not go out and explore the Amazon River (goal #2), but he could work to become an Eagle Scout (goal #71), which developed the skills in camping and boating he would use later to explore the Amazon. He started acting—right away—on those things he could do, and he did become an Eagle Scout. What action *do you* need to take right now to start this process in your life?

In grade school everything seemed to be telling me to give up on school. My report cards, my experience, my teacher's discouraging words, my lack of confidence, and my own negative attitude all pointed to the "fact" that I could never succeed in school. The whole situation made me angry, and the anger made me focus on a plan to change the "facts." Anger can be useful if you use it to become focused and determined. Calm down, harness that energy, and turn it in a positive direction.

My focus and positive energy brought an idea—an impossible dream—one outrageous goal—all A grades in high school, whatever it takes! My first small action was to start reading. It was the only thing I could think of at the time. Immediately taking some *action*, no matter how small, moves you from a daydream to a commitment. What *one goal* do you need to commit to right now? What *action* do you need to take today to move the dream to a commitment?

Is there someone you know who is already successful, who already is doing the things you would like to do in life, who might help you? Is there someone you know who might be a mentor for you—someone you can trust and talk to about helping you reach your goals? Why not contact them today—right now?

John Goddard did not achieve all of his goals. His original list contained one hundred twenty-seven goals (Appendix B). Of these, he actually achieved one hundred seventeen during his lifetime. But his achievements went well beyond his original list. For example, he not only landed and took off from an aircraft carrier (goal #73), but also set several jet aircraft speed records as a civilian test pilot.[86] When asked during an interview about how many of his goals he had achieved, he surprised the interviewer by saying that he had added many more goals since he wrote the original list at age fifteen; he said that he now had a list of six hundred goals, of which he had completed five hundred twenty.[87]

Goddard isn't the only one who didn't achieve all of his goals. I have a confession to make. I didn't achieve 100 percent of my *one goal* of making all A grades in high school. After my second year in high school, I took a summer math class at Indiana University High School, which was sixty miles from my home. My brother was a student at the university, and we roomed together in a boarding house just off campus. The high school was actually part of the university's education department. I was sixteen, loved being on my own away from home, and enjoyed the challenge of this environment, so I never went back home to school again. I graduated from Indiana University High School. With dramatically increased academic standards and enrolment in some University classes for high school credit, I did not make all A grades in high school. But I had improved so much in school because of my one goal that I had no trouble getting into college.

My *one goal* changed my life forever. It enabled me to dramatically improve my abilities in school, completely changed my group of friends to high achievers, and even changed my living environment—all in two years. Working toward achieving this *one goal* had created new opportunities I never dreamed of when I first committed to making all A grades in high school. Setting and achieving a few simple goals will open new opportunities for you, too.

If you set your goals high and don't achieve them 100 percent, you will still be better off than if you set no goals at all. Setting goals, making a plan, and taking *action* toward achieving those goals will change who you are. It will change how other people see you, and most importantly, *it will change how you see yourself.*

Achievement in life always leads to new opportunities. John Goddard didn't achieve all his goals on that original list, but the goals he did achieve led him to opportunities he never dreamed of at age fifteen—and John Goddard was a pretty good dreamer. Achieving *most* of my *one goal* made it possible for me to go to college; going to college made it possible for me to go to law school; going to law school opened up opportunities I never dreamed of at age fourteen when I set that *one goal.*

Maybe this all started at age eight, when I made a decision to stop chewing gum. It doesn't make any difference when you start setting goals—it just makes a difference that you make up your mind, commit, and take *action.* This is what it means to take charge of your own life. You set your own standards, make your own decisions, and commit to making them happen. As you overcome every obstacle in your path and refuse to give in to every person who opposes you, you will become strong. Once you start taking action, *don't stop!* Even if you fail, as everyone does, keep going. Don't give up, and in time you will succeed.

So, what is it that you want to do? What is the biggest impossible dream you can think of achieving? Is there a goal that is so exciting, so powerful, so life changing that you just know you have to try it? It is probably making you smile, just to think of it. What is it? Say it out loud. Write it down right now. *Take that first action to achieve a better life, because now you know how.*

YOU CAN DO THIS!

APPENDIX A

How to get help to improve your *reading,* *math,* and *writing:*

1. Go to the nearest public library and tell the person at the information desk that you need help learning reading, writing, or math. Don't stop asking until they find someone to help you—someone who can tell you about local programs and resources.

2. Most public libraries have computers you can use to find great learning programs for reading, writing, and math, free of charge.

3. If you are still in school, go to a guidance counselor or trusted teacher and tell them you need to improve in reading, writing, or math. Ask for their help, and work hard to follow their recommendations.

4. If you are out of school, go to your local library and follow steps 1 and 2 above. You can also ask someone in your community who is good at reading, writing, or math to help you improve your skills. Most people are willing to help someone who has a sincere desire to learn and improve.

5. If you are in prison, most state and federal prisons have guidance counselors who can tell you about learning programs at that location. Many prisons have excellent programs in reading, writing, and math. You can get GED and college training through local or online programs in almost all prisons.

Check out the following computer sites:
http://www.criminaljusticedegreesguide.com
https://www.prisonfellowship.org
www.literacyforincarceratedteens.org
http://www.finishyourdiploma.org

Check these sites on a computer for free help:

www.gcflearnfree.org—fun and easy programs for reading, writing, and math from the Goodwill Community Foundation

www.su24.maineadulted.org/contact/

And here is a great book for you:

The Millionaire's Secret by Tom Harkin (Thomas Nelson Publishers, 1998). If you struggle with reading, work on it by reading Tom's inspiring book.

APPENDIX B

John Goddard's List [88]

127 goals written at age fifteen (☑ indicates goal achieved)[*]

No.	Done ☑	Goal
EXPLORE		
1	☑	Nile River
2	☑	Amazon River
3	☑	Congo River
4	☑	Colorado River
5	☑	Yangtze River, China
6	☑	Niger River
7	☑	Orinoco River, Venezuela
8	☑	Rio Coco, Nicaragua
STUDY PRIMITIVE		
9	☑	The Congo
10	☑	New Guinea
11	☑	Brazil
12	☑	Borneo
13	☑	The Sudan
14	☑	Australia
15	☑	Kenya
16	☑	The Philippines
17	☑	Tanzania

18	☑	Ethiopia
19	☑	Nigeria
20	☑	Alaska
CLIMB		
21		Mt. Everest
22		Mt. Aconcagua, Argentina
23		Denali (Mt. McKinley)
24	☑	Mt. Huascaran, Peru
25	☑	Mt. Kilimanjaro
26	☑	Mt. Ararat, Turkey
27	☑	Mt. Kenya
28		Mt. Cook, New Zealand
29	☑	Mt. Popocatepetl, Mexico
30	☑	The Matterhorn
31	☑	Mt. Rainier
32	☑	Mt. Fuji
33	☑	Mt. Vesuvius
34	☑	Mt. Bromo, Java
35	☑	Grand Tetons
36	☑	Mt. Baldy, California
CAREER, STUDY, EXPERIENCE		
37	50%	Carry out careers in medicine & exploration
38	85%	Visit every country in the world (162 out of 192)
39	☑	Study Navaho & Hopi Indians
40	☑	Learn to fly a plane
41	☑	Ride a horse in Rose Parade
PHOTOGRAPH		
42	☑	Iguacu Falls, Brazil
43	☑	Victoria Falls, Rhodesia
44	☑	Sutherland Falls, New Zealand
45	☑	Yosemite Falls

APPENDIX B

46	☑	Niagara Falls
47	☑	Retrace travels of Marco Polo & Alexander the Great

EXPLORE UNDERWATER		
48	☑	Coral reefs of Florida
49	☑	Great Barrier Reef, Australia
50	☑	Red Sea
51	☑	Fiji Islands
52	☑	The Bahamas
53	☑	Explore Okefenokee Swamp & the Everglades

VISIT		
54		North and South Poles
55	☑	Great Wall of China
56	☑	Panama and Suez Canals
57	☑	Easter Island
58	☑	The Galapagos Islands
59	☑	Vatican City
60	☑	The Taj Mahal
61	☑	The Eiffel Tower
62	☑	The Blue Grotto
63	☑	The Tower of London
64	☑	The Leaning Tower of Pisa
65	☑	The Sacred Well of Chechen-Itza, Mexico
66	☑	Climb Ayers Rock in Australia
67		Follow River Jordan from Sea of Galilee to Dead Sea
68	☑	Lake Victoria
69	☑	Lake Superior
70	☑	Lake Tanganyika
71	☑	Lake Titicaca, South America
72	☑	Lake Nicaragua

ACCOMPLISH		
73	☑	Become an Eagle Scout
74	☑	Dive in a submarine
75	☑	Land and take off from an aircraft carrier
76	☑	Fly in a blimp, balloon, and glider
77	☑	Ride an elephant, camel, ostrich, and bronco
78	☑	Skin dive to 40 feet & hold breath 2.5 minutes underwater
79	☑	Catch a ten-pound lobster and a ten-inch abalone
80	☑	Play flute and violin
81	☑	Type 50 words a minute
82	☑	Make a parachute jump
83	☑	Learn water and snow skiing
84	☑	Go on a church mission
85	☑	Follow the John Muir trail
86	☑	Study native medicine and bring back useful ones
87	☑	Bag camera trophies of elephant, lion, rhino, cheetah, cape buffalo and whale
88	☑	Learn to fence
89	☑	Learn jujitsu
90	☑	Teach a college course
91	☑	Watch a cremation ceremony in Bali
92	☑	Explore depths of the sea
93		Appear in a Tarzan movie
94	60%	Own a horse, chimpanzee, cheetah, ocelot & coyote (didn't own chimp or cheetah)
95		Become a ham radio operator
96	☑	Build my own telescope
97	☑	Write a book
98	☑	Publish an article in National Geographic Magazine
99	☑	High jump five feet

APPENDIX B

100	☑	Broad jump 15 feet
101	☑	Run a mile in five minutes
102	☑	Weigh 175 pounds stripped
103	☑	Perform 200 sit-ups and 20 pull-ups
104	☑	Learn French, Spanish and Arabic
105		Study dragon lizards on Komodo Island
106	☑	Visit birth place of Grandfather Sorenson in Denmark
107	☑	Visit birth place of Grandfather Goddard in England
108	☑	Ship aboard a freighter as a seaman
109	80%	Read the entire Encyclopedia Britannica
110	☑	Read the Bible cover to cover
111	☑	Read the works of Shakespeare, Plato, Aristotle, Dickens, Thoreau, Rousseau, Conrad, Hemingway, Twain, Burroughs, Tallmadge, Tolstoy, Longfellow, Keats, Poe, Bacon, Whittier, and Emerson.
112	☑	Become familiar with the compositions of Bach, Beethoven, Debussy, Ebert, Mendelssohn, Lalo, Liszt, Rimsky-Korsakov, Respighi, Rachmaninoff, Paganini, Stravinsky, Tausch, Tchaikovsky, and Verdi
113	☑	Become proficient in the use of a plane, motorcycle, tractor, surfboard, rifle, pistol, canoe, microscope, football, basketball, bow and arrow, lariat, and boomerang.
114	☑	Compose music
115	☑	Play Clair de Lune on the piano
116	☑	Watch fire walking ceremony
117	☑	Milk a poisonous snake
118	☑	Light a match with a .22 rifle
119	☑	Visit a movie studio
120	☑	Climb Cheops' pyramid

121	☑	Become a member of the Explorer's Club and the Adventurer's Club
122	☑	Learn to play polo
123	☑	Travel through Grand Canyon on foot and by boat
124	☑	Circumnavigate the globe (did it four times)
125		Visit the moon (remember, he wrote this list in <u>1940</u>)
126	☑	Marry and have children (married with six children)
127	☑	Live to see the 21st century

APPENDIX C

LIFE GOALS: Example 1

YOUNG PERSON STILL IN SCHOOL

What I will achieve in the next 12 months

(Print in italics are author's examples)

HEALTH

- ❖ EXERCISE: *What are my exercise goals? How many times a week? (If you are playing a sport, what do you need to do to keep in shape for that sport?)*
- ❖ DIET: *Weight in lbs. (you set the goal)*
- ❖ MEDICATIONS: *Daily multivitamin, are there any medications you need to list?*
- ❖ OTHER: *Annual dental exams/cleanings, needed eye exams*

PERSONAL RELATIONSHIPS

- ❖ FAMILY: *How will I improve relationships with my family this year?*
- ❖ FRIENDS: *I will work at developing greater friendship(s) with . . . (list)*
- ❖ PERSONAL SKILLS: *I will develop skills in these sports . . . (list), I will develop my ability with guitar, violin, speaking, language skills, art . . . I will achieve the following in scouting skills/badges . . .*

SCHOOL

- ❖ COURSES: *I want to take the following classes this year:*
- ❖ GRADES: *My goals for grades this year are . . .*
- ❖ CAREERS: *Right now I think I want a career as . . . I will talk to the following people about this career goal:*

❖ ACTIVITIES: *I will take an active role in the following school activities:*

COMMUNITY ACTIVITIES
❖ CHURCH: *I will attend church services at. . . / I will join a Sunday school class*
❖ COMMUNITY: *I will be active in _____ this year and achieve the following:*

SPIRITUAL DEVELOPMENT
❖ OBJECTIVE: *My objective for this year is . . .*

WORK
❖ WHERE: *I will work at the following job / XX hours per week:*
❖ WHAT: *I will learn and accomplish the following things from my work:*
❖ OBJECTIVES: *What will be the positive results from my work? What do I expect to receive in return from this effort?*

FINANCIAL PLAN
❖ SAVINGS PLAN: *I will save $XXX this year to be used for (college?)*

ODDS AND ENDS (no time limit on achieving these)
❖ *Read at least one book each month for fun*
❖ *Drawing, painting, biking, swimming, skiing, golf, fishing, dance class*

ULTIMATE ACCOMPLISHMENTS (no time goal on these)
❖ *Own and run my own restaurant*
❖ *Make it to the state finals in . . .*
❖ *Climb Mt. Kilimanjaro in Africa*
❖ *Swim the English Channel*
❖ *Drive in a NASCAR race*
❖ *Help develop a cure for . . .*
❖ *Earn a college degree in . . .*

- *Travel to the following countries / places . . .*
- *Participate in the Olympics*
- *Raise and care for the following animals . . .*
- *Scuba dive in every ocean*
- *Help another person to get an education*
- *Be independently wealthy by the age of . . .*
- *Speak the following language(s)*
- *Sail my own boat to . . .*
- *Learn to . . .*
- *Read the works of . . .*
- *Write and publish a book about . . .*

LIFE GOALS: Example 2

YOUNG ADULTS:
What I will achieve in the next 12 months
(Print in italics are author's examples)

HEALTH
- EXERCISE: *Five (5) days/wk., run 12–15 miles/wk., weights 2 days/wk., one 10K/yr.*
- DIET: *Reduce sugar, weight 160± 2 lbs., cholesterol ≤ 190*
- MEDICATIONS: *Medications, multivitamin*
- OTHER: *Annual physical, annual dental exams/cleanings, ophthalmologist exams*

PERSONAL RELATIONSHIPS
- FAMILY (Or spouse): *time to talk each day, two-week vacation each year, family vacation at beach / Easter & Thanksgiving with wife's family.*

- ❖ FATHER: *Demonstrate love, spiritual strength, personal growth, continuous learning, honesty, integrity, responsibility, balance and joy in life that my children may learn by example and experience. (Children follow examples; they learn from what you DO, not just what you say), Take each child on a long weekend (just the two of us) each year*
- ❖ PARENTS: *Patience / manage their caregivers, medical needs, and finances so they can continue living in their home.*
- ❖ FRIENDS: *Work at developing deeper friendship with . . . list.*
- ❖ BUSINESS ASSOCIATES: *Develop deeper business friendship with . . . list.*
- ❖ PERSONAL SKILLS: *Guitar, golf, speaking opportunities, language skills.*

SPIRITUAL DEVELOPMENT
- ❖ OBJECTIVE: *Knowledge and understanding of scriptural principles*
- ❖ METHOD: *Pray for guidance earlier on issues of concern, devotional reading five days/wk., teach middle/high school Sunday school class*

COMMUNITY ACTIVITIES
- ❖ CHURCH: *Teach Sunday school class this year*
- ❖ BOARDS: *List boards and organizations in which you plan to be an ACTIVE participant*

LOCATION (where will you live)
- ❖ *City and State*

WORK
- ❖ WHERE: *what organization and what location*
- ❖ WHAT: *in my work this year I intend to accomplish the following . . .*
    1. _____
    2. _____
- ❖ OBJECTIVES: *What will be the positive results for the organization? What do I expect to receive in return from this effort?*

148

❖ BUSINESS SKILLS: *I will develop the following skills this year:*

LEISURE
❖ VACATION: *two-week vacation with family at beach*
❖ HOBBIES: *Woodworking (finish building shop)*
❖ SPORTS: *Golf (drop 2 strokes), one 10K race, ski, hike, fish*
❖ TRAVEL: *Florida beach, Colorado ski*

FINANCIAL PLAN
❖ Family budget / Financial Projection *(attached)*

ODDS AND ENDS (no time limit on achieving these)
❖ *Develop writing skills / write and publish a book*
❖ *Read at least one book per month*
❖ *Drawing, painting, build wood sail boat*
❖ *Develop speaking skills / speak with top national speakers*
❖ *Travel throughout the USA, Europe, Africa, South America*
❖ *Climb Mt. Kilimanjaro / climb all of the Colorado 14,000 peaks / hike in Himalayas*
❖ *Salmon fish in Alaska / hunt deer and turkey*
❖ *Time: to play golf, ski, enjoy nature with family and friends*

APPENDIX D

Resources
(Many of these resources are available at your public library)

HELP FROM DAVE RAMSEY /books

www.daveramsey.com/store/books/eBooks.html

Total Money Makeover (Thomas Nelson, 2013)

Smart Money Smart Kids, with Rachel Cruze (Ramsey Press, 2014)

Financial Peace Planner (Penguin Books, 1998)

More Than Enough (Penguin Books, 2002)

(Many of Dave Ramsey's materials are available in Audio, MP3, and DVD format. Dave Ramsey provides live audience seminars and the Total Money Makeover course is taught at many churches and civic organizations throughout the country.)

HELP EXPLORING FAITH/www.tremendouslifebooks.com
- ❖ Recommended: *Teen Life Application Study Bible*, New Living Translation (Tyndale House Publishers)
  Read: Mathew, Mark, Luke, John, and Acts
- ❖ *Life Is Tremendous* by Charles "Tremendous" Jones
  (for this and other books and recordings by Charlie Jones, go to: www.TremendousLifeBooks.com)
- ❖ *Student's Gold* (Honor Books, 1993)
- ❖ *One-Minute Pocket Bible for Teenagers* (Wisdom International, Inc., 2013)
- ❖ *More Than Just a Carpenter* by Josh D. McDowell and Sean McDowell (Tyndale Momentum, 2009)
- ❖ *The Power of Positive Thinking* by Norman Vincent Peale (Touchstone, 2003)

HELP FROM OTHER AUTHORS

- ❖ *The Millionaire Next Door: The Surprising Secrets of America's Wealthy* by Thomas J. Stanley, PhD, and William D. Danko, PhD (Taylor Trade Pub., 2010)
- ❖ *The New One-Minute Manager* by Ken Blanchard and Spencer Johnson, MD (William Morrow, 2015)
- ❖ *Grit: the Power of Passion and Perseverance* by Angela Duckworth (Scribner, 2016)
- ❖ *Business by the Book* by Larry Burkett (Thomas Nelson, 2006)
- ❖ *The Marshmallow Test* by Walter Mischel (Back Bay Books, 2015)

HELP IN OVERCOMING FEAR AND DISABILITIES

- ❖ *How to Win over Worry* by John Edmund Haggai (Harvest House, 2009)
- ❖ *Fractured Not Broken, a memoir* by Kelly Craig Schaefer and Michelle Weidenbenner *(Kelly Schaefer LLC, 2015)*
- ❖ *START: Punch Fear in the Face* by Jon Acuff (Ramsey Press, 2013)

HELP WITH PARENTING

- ❖ *Parenting with Love and Logic* by Foster Cline and Jim Fay (NavPress, 2006)
- ❖ *Love and Logic Magic for Early Childhood: Practical Parenting from Birth to Six Years* by Jim Fay and Charles Fay PhD (Love and Logic Press, 2000)

HELP FROM THE NATIONAL FATHERHOOD INITIATIVE

- ❖ **Father Facts** *7* /available FREE OF CHARGE online at www. fatherhood.org. This is the best research available on the effects of father absence and the importance of father involvement. *Father Facts 7* is the premier reference manual for anyone interested in promoting responsible involved fatherhood.

APPENDIX D

ENCOURAGING MOVIES BASED ON REAL-LIFE STORIES

❖ *October Sky*, starring Jake Gyllenhaal and Laura Dern (Universal Studios, 1999). Best Family Film, 1999. Based on the book *The Rocket Boys* by Homer Hickam Jr. (Dell/Random House, 1999).

❖ *The Pursuit of Happyness*, starring Will Smith (Columbia Pictures, 2006).

BOOKS BY JOHN GODDARD

❖ *Kayaks Down the Nile* by John Goddard (Brigham Young University Press, 1979)

❖ *The Survivor* by John Goddard (Health Communications, Inc., 2001)

AUTHOR'S NOTE: HOW TO LOOK UP A BIBLE VERSE

When I looked into the Christian faith I didn't know much about the Bible; in fact, I didn't even know how to look up a verse from a Bible reference. I have since found that many people don't know this, so here is how you do it. Below is the Bible reference for the "Story of Joseph" and directions on how to look it up in a Bible. This is a great story about a guy who had a very rough life but never gave up and finally succeeded.

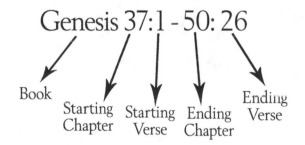

There are sixty-six books in the Bible (thirty-nine Old Testament and twenty-seven New Testament). Go to the index at the front of the Bible and look up the list of books of the Bible. Each <u>book</u> is listed with a page number. Find the <u>book</u> of "Genesis" (it's in the Old Testament). Go to the page number for Genesis. This page number will take you to the first page of the first <u>chapter</u> of Genesis. Page through the book of Genesis. The <u>chapter</u> numbers are the large bold ones, which appear on the left side of each column of print. At the <u>beginning</u> of each <u>verse</u> (or sentence), there is a little number, the <u>verse</u> number. <u>Verse</u> numbers always start over with "1" at the beginning of each <u>chapter</u>. That's all there is to it. Now you have the tools to explore God's Word.*

---

* (Reprinted from "Discipleship" by John Segal, ©November 1996)

APPENDIX E

More about the American Welfare System

In 1945, right after World War II, about 35 percent of all Americans were living at or below the poverty line. But that was soon to change, because American industry was on the upswing. The war had destroyed most of the industries in other countries, leaving the U.S. as practically the only strong economy left in the world—and business is a lot easier when you don't have much competition!

The fast-growing American economy created plenty of jobs, and competition for employees kept wages climbing. By 1964, only 19 percent of Americans were living at or below the poverty line.[89] In less than twenty years, with almost no government help, the percentage of poor Americans had dropped to almost half its postwar level.

HOW THE WELFARE SYSTEM WAS CREATED

Lyndon Johnson, the President of the United States in 1964, held the popular notion that we could rid America of all poverty through welfare legislation—a concept known as "The War on Poverty."[90] The reasoning was that if the percentage of Americans in poverty had dropped from 35 percent to 19 percent in only twenty years, surely the remaining 19 percent could get out of poverty with some government help.

Today, over fifty years later, it is estimated that our government has spent at least $19 trillion dollars ($19,000,000,000,000) to fight the "War on Poverty"[91]—by far, the largest government expenditure for the poor in the history of the world. One might expect that the percentage of people in poverty would drop to nearly zero. But in 2014 the reported percentage of Americans remaining in poverty was 14.3 percent.[92] After spending so much to fight poverty, why is this percentage still so high?

There are two reasons for this. First, the government bases the percentage on what Americans earn *before* including the government benefits they receive. The 14.3 percent number is actually the number of people who *qualify* for welfare before receiving any government benefits. In America, the percentage of people who are considered "poor" includes people who receive enough welfare that it would put their income over the poverty line if all of that welfare was included as income.

Second, when discussing welfare, our government only counts actual cash payments made to the poor. They don't include the value of "non-cash" items such as food stamps (SNAP), free or subsidized housing, Medicare or Medicaid, and many other items. [93]

If the government counted *as income* all the cash *and* non-cash benefits given to welfare recipients, it is generally agreed that the *real* percentage of "poor" Americans (those who *actually* live in poverty) would go way down [94] —as low as 2 or 3 percent.[95] This is being done by transferring huge amounts of money and benefits to the poor. These are expensive programs, but they have been largely *successful* at dramatically reducing the number of Americans who actually live in conditions of poverty.

The problem is that the welfare system does not have clear objectives for moving people off welfare rolls to a secure, *unsubsidized*, middle-class life, let alone programs capable of achieving these results. Our welfare system is an income and benefits *maintenance* program, designed (however unintentionally) to *keep* people in poverty. This is why it continues to grow. But can welfare continue to expand forever? With our huge national debt and declining funding for Social Security and Medicare, one has to wonder if our welfare programs will be sustainable in future decades.

When President Johnson announced the War on Poverty, he said, "Our aim is not only to relieve the symptoms of poverty but to cure it and, above all, to prevent it."[96] While the symptoms have been addressed, there has been little "cure" or "prevention." Our poorest citizens—as well as our taxpayers—deserve better. America needs focused programs dedicated to the *cure* and *prevention* of poverty, and we need to encourage the expansion of free enterprise to insure a robust, job-producing economy.

As I noted in the chapter "How Poverty Works," some of the problems in the current system stem from the fact that benefits are "means tested"—the more you work, the fewer benefits you receive. This is also true of savings.[97]

If you try to keep your expenses down and save every dime, the government cuts your welfare benefits, because you have too much in "assets" (under government rules, assets include cash savings, equity in a home or car, and the value of a small business you may have started). If you work hard and earn more, they cut your welfare; if you live simply and save, they cut your welfare. On the other hand, the system has no penalty for going into debt. You can borrow as much money as you want and go deeply into debt without affecting your welfare benefits.[98]

A major reason that many people are on welfare in America is the dramatic increase in single parents with small children.[99] This fact was covered in some detail in the "How Poverty Works" chapter. Programs to help poor single parents with small children have supported out-of-wedlock births and discouraged marriage. There can be little doubt that this has contributed to the normalization of single parenthood in our poorer communities, where the most dramatic cultural transformation has taken place.[100]

People don't get on welfare because they are lazy and don't want to work.[101] Many fall into the system because it seems like the only option. They aren't lazy, but they aren't stupid either. It is human nature to respond to incentives, and all the incentives created by the welfare system are negative. Our welfare system is structured to increase benefits to those who break all the rules for staying *out* of poverty. Welfare pays more money if you get pregnant, if you have additional children, if you stay single, if you are unemployed, if your child is diagnosed with asthma or ADHD, if you get divorced, if you don't save too much, and if you don't build assets.[102]

It is easy to become comfortable with a familiar situation, and difficult to generate the energy required to reach the dreams we held in our youth. The burden of raising small children without a partner to share the work and expenses, the lack of education from dropping out of school to care for these children, the poor schools, and the dangerous neighborhoods are huge barriers keeping people poor and dependent.

The fact that you lose benefits rapidly when you start working your way out of poverty has been described as the *poverty cliff*. Following the rules to stay out of poverty pushes you off the cliff. As you start to do better on your own, your benefits drop. The chart below shows you just how steep that cliff can be.

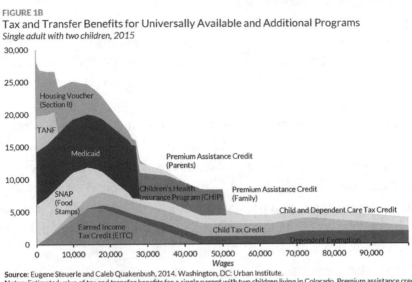

FIGURE 1B
Tax and Transfer Benefits for Universally Available and Additional Programs
Single adult with two children, 2015

Source: Eugene Steuerle and Caleb Quakenbush, 2014. Washington, DC: Urban Institute.
Notes: Estimated value of tax and transfer benefits for a single parent with two children living in Colorado. Premium assistance credit excludes the value of penalties paid by employers on the beneficiaries' behalf and the value of additional cost-sharing subsidies. Health coverage and quality of services provided varies by source: Medicaid and CHIP benefits are more comprehensive and have less cost-sharing than those in the exchange. Medicaid and CHIP also pay providers for services at lower rates than private insurers.

In 1996, Congress passed welfare reform legislation, which mandated "work requirements" in order to qualify for benefits. However, only 42 percent of adult welfare recipients are actually *working*.[103] Many recipients perform "work-related activities" that qualify as "work" under the welfare laws, such as job training, continuing education, and looking for a job. States are also allowed "hardship exemptions" for up to 20 percent of their welfare recipients. It is estimated that less than 20 percent of adult welfare recipients have unsubsidized private-sector jobs.[104]

The welfare system is extremely complicated, with at least eighty separate Federal programs and seven different Federal agencies designated to help low-income families. They often overlap and duplicate each other, are poorly coordinated, and are difficult to administer.[105] No single coordinated, central authority or control exists, and no single set of eligibility requirements is provided by the Federal agencies that administer these programs.[106] State, county, and municipal governments offer additional programs, further complicating the welfare landscape.

It is extremely difficult to compare benefits received in one state to those received in another. The primary Federal programs (TANF, SNAP, Housing, Medicaid, WIC, and LIHEAP) vary widely in the value of benefits provided because they differ in every state.[107] Welfare agencies judge their performance and base their budgets on the number of people they provide benefits to, not the number they move out of dependence and off the welfare rolls.

A massive and costly bureaucracy, with branches in every community in the nation, is needed to deal with this complexity.[108] Benefits change dramatically if you move to another state, get married, have additional children, have a child reaching age six or eighteen, have an elderly parent in residence, get a job, change your job, change the number of hours you work, serve in the military, have "special needs" children, complete or discontinue your education—and on, and on, and on. The complex differences between states is a substantial barrier that hinders the poor from relocating in search of more plentiful and higher-paying jobs.

Our government spends a lot on "income maintenance" programs and very little on programs to escape poverty.[109] It is well known that these programs discourage work, mobility, marriage, and savings.[110] This isn't because our government hates poor people; it's because the system is a patchwork of unconnected programs with no goals for improving the situation. They were stuck together over many years without any clear plan to help people develop the knowledge, skills, and requirements to move out of poverty.

There are many good ideas on how to fix these government programs, such as those outlined in the Economic Mobility Project.[111] There are also successful private initiatives, such as those of the Woodson Center (woodsoncenter.org) and the National Fatherhood Initiative (fatherhood. org), working to help poor communities. Circles USA (http://www. circlesusa.org/) has developed an innovative and effective program that brings community volunteers into partnership with families who are committed to getting out of poverty. Solutions to poverty are available if we, as a nation, will commit to making them work.

Previous attempts to fix the problems with welfare include the Welfare Reform Act of 1996, signed by President Clinton after he vetoed two previous bills; it had very positive results. In the years following this legislation, "welfare rolls plummeted by more than 60 percent, and the Congressional Budget Office reported that from 1991 to 2005, poor families with children saw their inflation-adjusted incomes climb by 35 percent, as employment climbed."[112] However, this decline in welfare was offset in part by an inverse rise in the number of low-income people on disability (a program which states have used to shift welfare costs back to the federal government).[113] Many provisions of the Welfare Reform Act of 1996 have been reversed in recent years. If you are trying to stay out of poverty now, it isn't likely that any plans to "fix" our welfare system will be done in time to help *you*.

The structure of our welfare system is discouraging, not only to those receiving benefits, but also to those working in agencies providing benefits, who carry heavy caseloads of poor families. The system is so debilitating that some give up the fight—they lose hope, they never get off welfare, and they never get above minimum living standards. They lack the job experiences that make them more valuable to employers, so they can't advance in life. Their dreams of a better life for themselves and their children are buried under mounds of government rules, bureaucratic red tape, social worker reports, and family court requirements. They are stuck in the trap of welfare poverty.

Don't let this happen to you and your family. There is a way out: follow the six goals explained in this book. They are simple, but not easy—and that's what makes them worthwhile, because achieving them will grow you into the complete person you were always meant to be.

YOU CAN DO THIS!

QUESTIONS & TOPICS
FOR DISCUSSION

PREFACE
1. Where are your best opportunities for a career with good income—sports, construction, medicine, business, or something else? Why?
2. How did the author come up with the six "rules"?

PART I: PAST AND PRESENT
1. What is the welfare system "trap"?
2. How did Shiana and Marik fall into the "trap"?
3. Did Shiana and Marik have a good relationship? Did they have a good plan? Was the baby "an accident"?
4. If Shiana finally gets her GED and a nursing degree, why would she continue to be poor?

PART II: POOR

RULE 1: PREGNANCY
1. Who must take responsibility for these rules? Who will try to stop you?
2. What is rule 1? Why does the author say it is the *first* and most *important* rule?
3. If you are young, unmarried, and have a baby, how does that increase your chances of being poor?
4. Do you think most pregnancies of young, unmarried people are an accident? Why or why not?
5. In a relationship, whose responsibility is it to protect against pregnancy? Why?
6. What is the "special order" for doing things in your life to stay out of poverty? Why does this make a difference?
7. LIFE CHOICE CHARTS: What is the first and most important thing you need to move from the Weak Life Plan to the Strong Life Plan? Why is it most important?

8. Do you think it is easier for children to grow up with two parents or with a single parent? Why?

RULE 2: WORK
1. How could working at a low-level job help you out of poverty? What helps you to get higher-level work?
2. Does the author want you to work in the fast-food industry, or is that just an example of a starting level job? What are some other starting level jobs you could get?
3. If welfare gives you as much money as working, why work?
4. How do the following things hold you back and how do you overcome them?
    1) Poor reading, writing, and math skills
    2) Addictions
    3) Poor attitude
    4) Disabilities
    5) Irrational fears?

RULE 3: MARRIAGE
1. Why would marriage help you stay out of poverty?
2. Wouldn't it be just as good to live together and share expenses? How would this affect children? What happens to property if one person in an unmarried relationship dies? What happens to the children?
3. What should you do if you are in a physically or psychologically abusive relationship?
4. Do you think religious faith could make a difference in your marriage?
5. What actions can you take to improve your chances of getting a good marriage partner?

PART III: SMART
1. What would your life be like if it was "rich and abundant"? List what you would want for such a life.

RULE 1: WORK SMART
1. Is it better to work to reach the standards set for you by others or your own high standards? Why or why not?

2. The author says, "When you *take* responsibility for something, it *gives* you control." What does he mean by that? Do you think it is true?

3. What was the one goal the author set when he started high school? Why do you think he succeeded with his "one goal"? What did he change to achieve it?

4. How did the author turn his anger into a positive force? Do you think you could do this? Have you ever done it?

5. How much education do you think you will need to stay out of poverty and reach a "rich and abundant" life?

6. Are you getting work experience right now that you might be able to use to reach a better life in the future? If not, what could you do to get such experience?

7. Do you have a "mentor"—a person who is successful at something you want to do who will help you learn? How could you find someone like that and contact them?

8. What is "capital equipment" and how does it become a "capital asset" which allows you to grow your wealth? Why does having "capital assets" give you advantages over just having a job and a salary?

9. How do good (and bad) small habits make a big impact on your life? What are your good habits? Do you have some habits you want to change?

10. Have you ever tried to overcome a fear? If there is something holding you back, what is your plan to overcome it?

RULE 2: SET GOALS

1. What are the "three key facts" that made Goddard's list amazing? Why are those important for setting goals?

2. Have you done the three exercises for writing down your life goals? Why or why not? If not, when will you do them?

RULE 3: SEEK GOD

1. The author describes a bad experience he had when he first went to church with his parents. Have you had any experiences like that? How has your experience with church or religion affected your faith?

2. Why couldn't the author find "proof" for the Christian faith? Did he find "evidence"?

3. Are your decisions about faith based on what your parents taught you, or are they your own?

4. What does the author say you should read before making up your mind about Jesus Christ?

PART IV: RICH
1. Is money an important part of a "rich and abundant" life? How does having money give you more choices in life?
2. Do most millionaires in America inherit their money?
3. What is "Wealth Attitude"?
4. What do people who get wealthy do with the money they have left over at the end of the month?
5. What is "delayed gratification"? Have you ever used this in your life? Is this a "natural" skill or one you can learn and improve?
6. What is "grit"? Is "grit" something you are born with or can you develop it with practice?
7. What is "wealth"? Is it an amount of money? Do wealthy people go into debt to get what they want?
8. What does it mean to become "financially independent"?
9. Could you start your own business? What would it be?

ACTION
1. Have you taken any action to improve your life based on something you read in this book? Why or why not?

ACKNOWLEDGMENTS

Special thanks to Dana Lane. After business demands on my time caused me to stop teaching young people for several years, Dana asked if I would give that instruction to her home-schooled teens. After I did that she asked if I would give the class to the young people in her church. I had always intended to put these lessons into a book but it was Dana's requests which sparked action.

Since I had taught these materials for many years, I thought it would be easy to transfer my notes and outlines into a book. Three and a half years later, I have come to understand that writing a book is a far more difficult and complicated task. I am greatly indebted to many people for helping me through this process. They are, in no particular order:

The wonderful team at Tremendous Leadership for encouragement and direction. Tracey Jones, who leads that great team, along with Ronda Ranalli and Kelly McGinley, helped to direct my efforts and hone my message. Many thanks to David Fessenden for editing which helped me understand the difference between spoken words and written language, and Marjorie Vawter who helped me learn some grammar I missed in school as well as proper footnoting.

Sara Diehl, entrepreneur and owner of Empire Coaching, made my writing look like a book for the first time. Her own life story of overcoming poverty and moving from poor, to smart, to rich is testament to the ideas presented in this book. Author and Olympian Rubén González provided publishing contacts and clear, tough-minded advice on writing and book development. Two talented writers and great friends, Don and Sheryl Eberly, provided very early insight regarding structure and content. After hearing the story of my early life, they encouraged me to include these events which greatly changed the tone and direction of this book.

Many friends, business associates and former students took time to read various drafts. I am greatly indebted for the insights, corrections and comments they provided. They include: Chris Brown, Doug Bawel, Joe

Buehler, Evan Burns, Abby Dawkins, John and Charlotte Donan, Tom and Juanita Eckert, Landy Gabhart, Jeffery Goddard, James and Kaye Griffin, Richard and Kathy Hines, Ryan and Blayr Kramer, Greg and Sara Krodel, Vann, Dana, Shelby and Josh Lane, Jamie Levy, Ronnie McBrayer, David Nixon, Randy Norris, Terry and Dianne Olive, Brad and Tara Popp, Robert and Lovella Ruckriegel, Shawn and Kelly Schaefer, Bill and Laurie Schwarz, Kevin and Denise Simonson, Lavonne Segal, Andy Staples, Gary and Danita Brick, Glen Sturm, John Smith and Dr. Martha Yearsley. Thanks also to the many bright young people I have had the privilege to teach, from Sunday school through graduate school—I hope you have benefited as much as I have.

I owe so much to my family. Thanks to my parents, Arthur and Mildred, who struggled mightily in life and thankfully lived long enough for us to share a deep and abiding love. Many thanks to my brother and business partner, Steve—we have journeyed together since childhood, from poor, to smart, to rich, defending and protecting each other through more difficulties than either of us cares to remember. We stayed the course; we won the fight.

Thanks to my sons, Jason and Michael, who listened to me teach the lessons in this book countless times. You are the greatest blessings any mother and father could ask. Last, but certainly not least, my beloved wife Sara, who has read each draft and applied her IBM Communications Manager skills to correct, edit, revise and support my writing efforts at every turn. I love being with you and enjoy our adventures together. You make my life so complete and fulfilling.

NOTES

PART I

1.   U.S. Dept. of Health and Human Services (HHS), 2017 Poverty Guidelines. The threshold money income level for defining poverty is set annually by the U.S. Census Bureau and varies slightly from the HHS Guidelines. The dollar amounts listed here are for the forty-eight contiguous states and the District of Columbia (guidelines for Alaska and Hawaii are slightly higher). Many U.S. government agency aid programs use different poverty measures. Amounts shown are 100 percent of Federal Poverty Level (FPL). See https://aspe.hhs.gov/poverty-guidelines chart of all available FPLs.

2.   Eugene C. Steuerle, "Labor Force Participation, Taxes, and the Nation's Social Welfare System" (statement and testimony given at the U.S. House of Representatives, hearing before the Committee on Oversight and Government Reform, 114th Cong., 1st sess., February 14, 2013). https://oversight.house.gov/wpcontent/uploads/2013/02/Steuerle-Testimony.pdf

     Author's note: The example here is simplified and uses rounded numbers for ease of understanding to illustrate the point that the marginal tax rate reduces the value trade-off between welfare and earned income. When moving from poverty to 150 percent of poverty, the trade-off is about 60 percent (59.2 percent simple average—see Table I of the cited study, which is based on welfare recipients receiving only TANF, SNAP, and Medicaid). The example is also intended to highlight the fact that this is not merely a dollar value exchange, but includes a significant loss of leisure (alternative use) time which is often underrated or left out of consideration altogether. This trade-off percentage varies widely by state, family composition, and services provided, in a normal range from 40 percent to 80 percent.

     Also see: Elaine Maag, C. Eugene Steuerle, Ritakhi Chakravarti, and Caleb Quakenbush, "How Marginal Tax Rates Affect Families at Various Levels of Poverty," *National Tax Journal* 65(4) (2012): 759–82. http://www. ntanet.org/NTJ/65/4/ntjv65n04p759-82-how-marginal-tax-rates.pdf

3.   Michael D. Tanner, "Why Get Off Welfare?," *Los Angeles Times* (Online), August 22, 2013, http://articles.latimes.com/2013/aug/22/opinion/la-oe-tanner-welfare-work-pay-20130822; also see Michael D. Tanner and Charles Hughes, "The Work Versus Welfare Trade-Off: 2013," Cato Institute, Table 15 "Welfare Benefits, Taxes and Pretax Wage Equivalents," 2013. https://www.cato.org/publications/white-paper/work-versus-welfare-trade

     Author's Note: In the *Los Angeles Times* article, Michael Tanner lists the value of a full package of welfare benefits in a medium-level welfare state as $28,500 (in 2013). Applying this to Table 15 of the Cato Institute study results in a 91.5 percent multiple in order to calculate the equivalent earned hourly wage of $25,996 or $12.50/hr. based

167

on a full-time work year of 2080 hours. The reduction in the equivalent earned income is due to the effect of earned income tax credits.

4. Ibid.

5. Tanner and Hughes, "The Work Versus Welfare Trade-Off: 2013," 2, 39–41.

   Author's Note: Although most state and federal welfare programs require that recipients work, there are many work "equivalents," such as continuing education, job training and looking for work, which fulfill the "work requirement." Less than 42 percent of welfare recipients are engaged in some form of work activity and less than 20 percent work in unsubsidized private-sector jobs.

6. Kay Hymowitz, Jason S. Carroll, W. Bradford Wilcox, and Kelleen Kaye, "Knot Yet: The Benefits and Costs of Delayed Marriage in America," a new report from the National Marriage Project, the National Campaign to Prevent Teen and Unplanned Pregnancy and the Relate Institute, March 15, 2013. http://twentysomethingmarriage. org/summary/. Barbara Ray, "Cohabitation's Effect on Kids: cohabitation in US is fragile and short, and likely hard on kids, research finds," *Psychology Today*, Posted March 19, 2013, https://www.psychologytoday.com/blog/ adulthood-whats-the-rush/201303/cohabitations-effectkids.

7. The story of Shiana and Marik is a composite example created from individual and group discussions with the author regarding the experience of young people who have dealt with out-of-wedlock childbirth early in life, as well as studies, interviews, and discussions from various research sources. Shiana and Marik are fictional names and characters. For a thorough, empathetic, and highly readable study and analysis of this subject see: Kathryn Edin and Maria Kefalas, *Promises I Can Keep, Why Poor Women Put Motherhood before Marriage,* (Berkeley, CA: University of California Press, 2011).

PART II

8. Walt DeNavas, Carmen and Bernadette D. Proctor, U.S. Census Bureau, Current Population Reports, P60-249, *Income and Poverty in the United States: 2013*, Table B-1, Poverty Status of People by Family Relationship, Race, and Hispanic Origin: 1959 2013 (All People) (Washington, DC: U.S. Government Printing Office, 2014). https:// www.census.gov/content/dam/Census/library/publications/ 2015/demo/p60-252.pdf.

9. Ibid.

   Author's Note: The federal government of the United States does not keep any records on the total cost of welfare programs created by the "War on Poverty." For a more detailed discussion regarding estimates of the total cost of these programs and the welfare system see Appendix E, The Welfare System.

10. Robert Rector, "Marriage: America's Greatest Weapon Against Child Poverty" (Washington, DC: The Heritage Foundation, September 16, 2010).

    The article's author based 80% calculations on the U.S. Bureau of the Census, American Community Survey, 2006. https://factfinder.census.gov/servlet/Dataset/ MainPageServlet?_program=ACS&_submenuled=datasets_ 2&_long=en. Also see

NOTES

Ron Haskins, "Combating Poverty: Understanding New Challenges for Families" (statement and testimony given at the U.S. Senate, hearing before the Finance Committee, 112th Cong., 2nd sess., June 5, 2012. "One of our arguments, based in part on a Brookings analysis of Census Bureau data, is that young people can virtually assure that they and their families will avoid poverty if they follow three elementary rules for success—complete at least a high school education, work full time, and wait until age 21 and get married before having a baby. Based on analysis of Census data, people who follow all three of these rules had only a 2 percent chance of being in poverty and a 72 percent chance of joining the middle class (defined as above $55,000 in 2010). These numbers were almost precisely reversed for people who violated all three rules, elevating their chances of being poor to 77 percent and reducing their chances of making the middle class to 4 percent. Individual effort and good decisions about the big events in life are more important than government programs." Also see Wendy Wang and W. Bradford Wilcox, "The Millennial Success Sequence: Marriage, Kids, and the "Success Sequence" among Young Adults", American Enterprise Institute, June 2017. Analysis based on the National Longitudinal Survey of Youth reports findings that 97 percent of those who earn at least a high-school diploma, work, and marry before having children will be out of poverty as they enter their 30's. www.aei.org/wp-content/uploads/2017/06/IFS-MillennialSuccessSequence-Final.pdf.

11. "Births Preliminary Data for 2008," (Center for Disease Control, National Center for Health Statistics, National Vital Statistics Report, April 10, 2010), Table 7. http://www.cdc.gov/nchs/data/nvsr/nvsr5816.pdf.

12. Ibid.

13. Sam Brownback and David Blankenhorn, "End the Welfare Marriage Penalty," *The Wall Street Journal* (updated May 13, 2008). http://www.wsj.com/articles/SB121063787788786833.

Author's Note: This article estimates the marriage penalty for welfare recipients to be 10–25 percent and recommends eliminating it for the first three years of marriage. Also see "Welfare Reform, Welfare Examples; Marriage Penalty Inherent in Welfare System," The Federal Safety Net. Based on 2011–2012 IRS, SNAP-USDA, and HUD statistics, this article illustrates comparative examples of how "means tested" welfare is a substantial discouragement to marriage for a single mother. http://federalsafetynet.com/welfare-examples.html

14. Kathryn Edin and Maria Kefalas, *Promises I Can Keep: Why Poor Women Put Motherhood before Marriage* (Berkeley: University of California Press, 2011); Paula England and Kathryn Edin, eds., *Unmarried Couples with Children* (New York: Russell Sage Foundation, 2009), 25–54. http://www.jstor.org/stable/10.7758/9781610441865

Also see Kathryn Edin, Paula England, Emily Fitzgibbons Shafer, and Joanna Reed, "Forming Fragile Families: Was the Baby Planned, Unplanned, or In Between?" Available at https://www.russellsage.org/publications

15. A. Sonfield and Rachel B. Gold, *Public Funding for Family Planning, Sterilization and Abortion Services, FY 1980–2010* (New York: Guttmacher Institute, 2012),

https://www.guttmacher.org/report/public-funding-familyplanning-sterilization-and-abortion-services-fy-1980-2010.

16. "Contraceptive Use in the United States," Contraception Effectiveness Fact Sheet, Guttmacher Institute, October 2015 / table source: Hatcher RA et al., eds., *Contraceptive Technology, 20th ed*ition (New York: Ardent Media, 2011).www.guttmacher.org/fact-sheet/contraceptive-use-united-states

17. The term "success sequence," was created by Brookings Institute scholars Ron Haskins and Isabel Sawhill, who first drew attention to a list of items which are strong predictors of upward economic mobility for young people. Since Haskins' and Sawhill's original "success sequence" list, various scholars and pundits have included and excluded items to create similar lists. In this text, the term "special order" is used to avoid confusion with prior lists, and to allow inclusion of items which encourage generational movement from poverty to middle class and beyond. See footnote 10 above.

18. Sara S. McLanahan, Irwin Garfinkel, Nancy Reichman, Julian Teitler, Marcia Carlson, and Christina Norland Audigier, "The Fragile Families and Child Wellbeing Study: Baseline National Report" (Princeton, NJ: Center for Research on Child Wellbeing, Princeton University, 2003).

Author's Note: Most single mothers believe it is best to marry before children and want to marry in the future. http://www.Fragilefamilies.princeton.edu/sites/fragilefamilies/files/nationalreport.pdf. United States census Bureau, U.S. Department of Commerce, Current Population Survey, "Marital Status of Residents of the United States of America," 2004: more than 80 percent of Americans have been married at some time in life. http://www.uttmacher.org/fact-sheet/contraceptive-use-united-states. Frank Newport and Joy Wilke, "Desire for Children Still Norm in U.S.," Gallup Poll, September 25, 2013: more than 90 percent of American adults either have children or say they want to have children. http://www.gallup.com/ poll/164618/desire-children-norm.aspx

19. Marcia J. Carleson, *"Trajectories of Couples' Relationship Quality after Child Birth: Does Marriage Matter?"* Center for Research on Child Wellbeing, Working Paper No. 2007-11-FF, April 2007. Also see Bendheim-Thoman Center for Research on Child Wellbeing. (2003). Union formation and dissolution in fragile families. Fragile Families Research Brief (Princeton, NJ: Princeton University, July 2002, Number 9).

20. The Child Support Enforcement Program, created by Title IV-D of the Social Security Act. http://www.acfhhs.gov/ programs/css/resource/fy2013-preliminary-report

21. U.S. Census Bureau, Historic Poverty Tables—Families, Table 4. Poverty Status by Type of Family, Presence of Related Children, All Races (Washington, DC, 2014). The poverty rate is lower in all married families, for racial classifications, than it is for single parent families regardless of sex of the parent. http://www.census.gov/ hhes/ www/poverty/data/historical/families.html.

Kyle Peterson, "The March of Foolish Things," Weekend Interview with Thomas Sowell, *Wall Street Journal* (Sept. 4, 2015). "For every year from 1994 to the present, black married couples have had a poverty rate in single digits." http://www.wsj.com/

articles/the-march-of-foolish-things-1441407396.

22. Jay D. Teachman, "Premarital Sex, Premarital Cohabitation, and the Risk of Subsequent Marital Dissolution among Women, *Journal of Marriage and Family* 65:444–455 (2003). Reprinted in J. Davidson, N. Moore and T. Fischer, eds., *Speaking of Sexuality: Interdisciplinary Reading* (Oxford University Press, 2009). http://www.jstor.org/stable/3600089. Also see D. T. Lichter, Z. Qian, "(2008)Serial Cohabitation and the Marital Life Course," *Journal of Marriage and Family* (2008), 70, 861878.

23. U.S. Census Bureau, *Children's Living Arrangements and Characteristics* (Washington D.C.: March 2011), Table C8. Children in father-absent homes are almost four times more likely to be poor. In 2011, 12 percent of children in married-couple families were living in poverty, compared to 44 percent of children in mother only families, http://www.fatherhood.org/father-absence-statistics.

24. Cynthia Osborne and Sara McLanahan, "Partnership Instability and Child Wellbeing," *Journal of Marriage and Family*, 69.4 (2007): 1065-1083k. Data from three waves of the Fragile Families Study (N=2,111) was used to examine the prevalence and effects of mothers' relationship changes between birth and age three on their children's well-being. Children born to single mothers show higher levels of aggressive behavior than children born to married mothers. Living in a single-mother household is equivalent to experiencing 5.25 partnership transitions. http://www.childandfamilyresearch.org/ research/family-instability/

25. Connee A. Bush PhD, Ronald L. Mullis PhD, and Ann K. Mullis PhD, "Differences in Empathy Between Offender and Non-Offender Youth," *Journal of Youth and Adolescence* (August 2000): 467-478. A study of 109 juvenile offenders indicated that family structure significantly predicts delinquency. https://www.ncjrs.gov/App/abstractdb/AbstractDBDetails.aspx?id=184359

26. Cynthia C. Harper and Sara S. McLanahan, "Father Absence and Youth Incarceration," Journal of Research on Adolescence, Vol.14, Issue 3 (September 2004): 369397. Even after controlling for income, youths in father-absent households still had significantly higher odds of incarceration than those in mother-father families. Youths who never had a father in the household experienced the highest odds of incarceration. http://onlinelibrary.wiley. com/doi/10.1111/j.15327795.2004.00079.x/abstract.

27. Jay D. Teachman, "The Childhood Living Arrangements of Children and the Characteristics of Their Marriages." Journal of Family, Issue 25 (January 2004): 86–111. Being raised by a single mother increases a child's risk of experiencing teen pregnancy, marrying without graduating from high school, and of forming a marriage or other relationship with both partners having less than a high school education. https://www.ncjrs.gov/App/Publications/ abstract.aspx?ID=184359

28. "CPS Involvement in Families with Social Fathers," Fragile Families Research Brief No. 46 (Princeton, NJ and New York, NY: *Bendheim-Thomas Center for Research on Child Well-being and Social Indicators Survey Center*), 2010. A study using data from the Fragile Families and Child Wellbeing Study revealed that in many cases the absence of a biological father contributes to increased risk of child maltreatment. The results suggest that Child Protective Services (CPS) agencies have some justification in

viewing the presence of a nonbiological (social) father as increasing children's risk of abuse and neglect. It is believed that in families with a nonbiological (social) father figure, there is a higher risk of abuse and neglect to children, despite the nonbiological (social) father living in the household or only dating the mother. http://www.fatherhood.org/why-fatherhood-matters Also see S. L. Brown and J. R. Bulanda (2008), "Relationship Violence in Young Adulthood: A Comparison of Daters, Cohabitors, and Marrieds," *Social Science Research* (2008), 37, 73–87; L. J. Waite and M. Gallagher, *The Case for Marriage* (New York: Doubleday, 2000).

29. U.S. Department of Labor, Bureau of Labor Statistics, *National Longitudinal Survey of Youth*, www.bls.gov/ nls/nlsy97.htm. The NLSY97 consists of a nationally representative sample of approximately 9,000 youths who were twelve to sixteen years old as of December 31, 1996. This survey found that obese children are more likely to live in father-absent homes than are non-obese children. http://www.bls.gov/nls/handbook/2005/nlshc2.pdf.

30. John P. Hoffmann and Felicia G. Cerbone, "The Community Context of Family Structure and Adolescent Drug Use," Journal of Marriage and Family, Issue 3, Vol. 66: 314–330, (2002). Even after controlling for community context, there is significantly more drug use among children who do not live with their mother and father. Also see Robert A. Johnson, John P. Hoffmann, and Dean R. Gerstein, "The Relationship Between Family Structure & Adolescent Substance Use," U.S. Gov. Printing Office (July 1996). https://scholar.google.com/citations?view_op=view_citation&hl=en&user=3j2TmR4AAAAJ&cstart=20&citation_for_view=3j2TmR4AAAAJ:vV6vV6tmYwMC.

31. U.S. Department of Education, National Center for Education Statistics, Fathers' and Mothers' Involvement in Their Children's Schools by Family Type and Resident Status (NCES 2001-032), Christine Winquist Nord and Jerry West, Washington, D.C. (2001). Father involvement in schools is associated with the higher likelihood of a student getting mostly As. This was true for fathers in biological parent families, for stepfathers, and for fathers heading single-parent families. http://nces.ed.gov/pubs 2001/2001032.pdf.

32. Paul A. Jargowsky, "Stunning Progress, Hidden Problems: The Dramatic Decline of Concentrated Poverty in the 1990s," The Living Cities Census Series, May 2003, The Brookings Institute. Also see Brett Drake and Mark R. Rank, "The Racial Divide Among American Children in Poverty: Reassessing the Importance of Neighborhood," *Children and Youth Services Review* 31:1264–1271.

33. U.S. Bureau of Labor, Bureau of Labor Statistics, Division of Occupational Employment Statistics, "Occupational Employment and Wages, May 2015, 35–3021 Combined Food Preparation and Serving Workers, Including Fast Food; Restaurants and Other Eating Places" (Washington, DC: May 2015). Hourly mean wage $9.15, at full time 2080 hours/year annual mean wage $19,032/year. https://www.bls.gov/home.htm

34. Irwin S. Kirsch, Ann Jungeblut, Lynn Jenkins, and Andrew Colstad, "Adult Literacy in America: A First Look at the Findings of the National Adult Literacy Survey" (Washington, D.C.: U.S. Department of Education, Office of Educational Research

and Improvement, National Center for Education Statistics, April 2002), NCES 1993-275. https://nces.ed.gov/pubs 93/93275.pdf

35. Ibid.

36. PBS, *Frontline*, "Dropout Nation," Corporation for Public Broadcasting in cooperation with American Graduate (September 25, 2012). The average dropout can expect to earn an annual income of $20,241, according to the U.S. Census Bureau (PDF). That is a full $10,386 less than the typical high school graduate, and $36,424 less than someone with a bachelor's degree. https://archive.org/details/WMPT_20120926_010000_Frontline. Analysis for this PBS special report was based on research by American Graduate studies of the Washington, D.C., school district:

37. Elizabeth Greenberg, Eric Dunleavy and Mark Kufner, *Literacy Behind Bars, Results from 2003 National Assessment of Adult Literacy Prison Survey* (U.S. Department of Education, National Center for Educational Statistics, American Institute for Research, May 2007), NCES 2007-473. http://nces.ed.gov/pubs2007/2007473.pdf

38. Irwin S. Kirsch, Ann Jungeblut, Lynn Jenkins, and Andrew Kolstad, *Adult Literacy in America; Findings of the National Adult Literacy Survey*, 3rd ed. (U.S. Department of Education, National Center for Education Statistics, Office of Educational Research and Improvement, National Assessment of Adult Literacy [NAAL], April 2002), NCES 1993-275.. https://nces.ed.gov/pubs93/93275.pdf.

39. National Institute on Drug Abuse, National Institute of Health, "Principles of Drug Addiction Treatment: A Research Based Guide (third edition)," December 2012. https://www.drugabuse.gov/publications/principles-drug addiction-treatment-research-based-guide-third-edition/principles-effective-treatment.

40. Ibid. Also see National Institute on Drug Abuse, National Institute of Health, "Emerging Trends," December 2015. https://www.drugabuse.gov/drugs-abuse/emerging-trends

41. Kelly Craig Schaefer with M. Weidenbenner, *Fractured Not Broken, A Memoir* (Kelly Schaefer LLC with R. Publishing LLC, 2015).

42. Jennifer Rubin, "The Poverty Issue Is about Marriage," *The Washington Post*, April 7, 2014. https://www. washingtonpost.com/blogs/right-turn/wp/2014/04/07/the-poverty-issue-is-about-marriage. Also see William Galston, "The Poverty Cure: Get Married," *Wall Street Journal*, October 27, 2015. http://www.wsj.com/articles/ the-poverty-cure-get-married-1445986205.

43. Marilyn Kasian and Susan L. Painter, "Frequency and Severity of Psychological Abuse in a Dating Population," Carleton University, September 1992. http://jiv.sagepub com/content/7/3/350.full.pdf+html. Also see David R. Jezl, Christian E. Molidor, and Tracy L. Wright, "Physical, Sexual, and Psychological abuse in high school dating relationships: Prevalence rates and self-esteem issues," *Child and Adolescent Social Work Journal*, February 1996, (Volume 13, Issue 1), 69–87. http://link.springer.com/article/10.1007/BF01876596.

44. Kristin Gavin, PhD., "Twelve Signs Your Partner is an Emotional Abuser," August 13, 2014. http://www.your tango.com/experts/dr-kristin-davin-psy-d/emotional-abuse. Also see Centers for Disease Control and Prevention (2014). "Intimate partner violence:

Definitions." https://www.cdc.gov/violenceprevention/intimatepartnerviolence/ definitions.html. Also see National Coalition Against Domestic Violence (NCADV) Facts About Domestic Violence and Psychological Abuse. www.ncadv.org.

45. D. Popenoe and B. D. Whitehead, "The State of our Unions 2007: The Social Health of Marriage in America" (Piscataway, NJ: The National Marriage Project, 2007), 18–19.

46. Linda Gorman, "Is Religion Good For You?" (The National Bureau of Economic Research). http://www.nber.org/digest/oct05/w11377.html

   Also see M. D. Bramlett and W. D. Mosher, "Cohabitation, Marriage, Divorce, and Remarriage in the United States," *Vital and Health Statistics*, 23 (22), (Hyattsville, MD: National Center for Health Statistics, 2002).

47. Dr. Wade F. Horn, PhD, "Take a Vow to Promote Benefits of Marriage," *The Washingon Post,* Nov. 7, 1999.

48. Carmen DeNavas, Walt and Bernadette D. Proctor, "Median Household Income: 2012 and 2013," *Income and Poverty in the United States: 2013*, P60-249, (Washington, DC: U.S. Government Printing Office, U.S. Census Bureau, Current Population Reports, 2014)

PART III

49. Ibid.

50. Mark Rank, Thomas A. Hirschl, and Kirk A. Foster, *Chasing the American Dream* (Oxford: Oxford University Press, April 2014), 96. There is greater income fluidity at the top of the income distribution scale. In the U.S., 76.8 percent of individuals will exceed $100,000 annual income and 20.6 percent will exceed $250,000 annual income. This segment is made up of diverse individuals generally having higher education levels, professional careers, often dual-couple incomes and residing in major metropolitan areas.

51. "Renewing the American Dream, a Roadmap to Enhancing Economic Mobility in America" (Washington, DC: Pew Charitable Trust, Economic Mobility Project, 2008). The Economic Mobility Project is a nonpartisan collaboration led by The Pew Charitable Trusts and comprised of a group of principals from five leading policy institutions: The American Enterprise Institute, The Brookings Institution, The Heritage Foundation, The New America Foundation, and The Urban Institute. The objective of the Economic Mobility Project is to provide the best available facts, figures, and trends in economic mobility and broadening the focus of the national economic debate to include an understanding of the health and status of the American Dream. Each of the project's principals believes that economic mobility plays a central role in defining the American experience and that more can and should be done to improve one's ability to move up the income ladder. Based on a shared commitment to renewing the American Dream, this road map presents a comprehensive set of nonpartisan policy ideas to enhance economic mobility. http://www.pewtrusts.org/en/research-and-analysis/reports/2009/11/06/renewing-the-american-dream-a-road-map-to-enhancing-economic-mobility-in-america

52. Diana Furchtgott-Roth, Louis Jacobson, and Christine Mokher, "Strengthening Community Colleges Influence on Economic Mobility" (Washington, DC: Pew Charitable Trust, Economic Mobility Project, 2008). http://www.frbsf.org/economicresearch/files/Jacobson.pdf.

53. Ibid.

54. Thomas J. Stanley and William D Danko, *The Millionaire Next Door* (Longstreet Press, 1996).

55. Ibid.

56. K. M. Flegal, M. D. Carroll, B. K. Kit, C. L. Ogden, "Prevalence of Obesity and Trends in the Distribution of Body Mass Index among US Adults, 1999–2010," *Journal of the American Medical Association*, (2012) 307(5): 491–97. Available online: http://jamanetwork.com/journals/ jama/fullarticle/1104933?resultClick=1.

   Author's Note: the term "overweight" refers to an excessive amount of body weight and "obesity" refers to an excess amount of body fat.

57. "State of American Well-Being, 2014 Obesity Rankings," released May 26, 2015, Gallop-Healthways Well-Being Index. http://www.healthways.com/previewwbi/2014-obesity-report-0

58. "Childhood Obesity Facts," last updated: June 19, 2015, http://www.cdc.gov/obesity/data/childhood.html.

59. Charles Duhigg, The Power of Habit: Why We Do What We Do in Life and in Business (New York: Random House, February 2012).

60. John E. Haggai, *How To Win Over Worry* (Harvest House Publications, 2001).

61. "One Man's Life of No Regrets," *Life Magazine*, vol. 72, no. 11, (Revised May 20, 2013) 66–68. https://books.com/books?id=elIEAAAAMBAJ&q=John+Goddard#v=snippet&q=John%20Goddard&f=false.

62. Chauncey Sanders, *Introduction In Research in English Literary History* (New York: Macmillian Co., 1952), 145. "There are now more than 5,300 known Greek manuscripts of the New Testament. Add over 10,000 Latin Vulgate and at least 9,300 other early versions (MSS) and we have more than 24,000 manuscript copies of portions of the New Testament in existence today. No other document of antiquity even begins to approach such numbers and attestation. In comparison, the *Iliad* by Homer is second with only 643 manuscripts that still survive. The first complete preserved text of Homer dates from the 13th century." Harold J. Greenlee, *Introduction to New Testament Textual Criticism* (Grand Rapids: William B Eerdmans Publishing Co., 1964), 15. "The earliest extant MSS of the New Testament were written much closer to the date of the original writing than is the case in almost any other piece of ancient literature." Also see, Josh McDowell, *Evidence That Demands a Verdict*, Vol. I (San Bernardino, CA: Hereslife Publishing Inc., 25th printing, June 1986).

63. Jerry Vardaman, "A New Inscription Which Mentions Pilate as 'Prefect,'" *Journal of Biblical Literature*, Vol. 81, (1962), 70–71. Also see A. N. Sherwin-White, review of

"A. Frova, L'iscrizione di Ponzio Pilato a Cesarea," *The Journal of Roman Studies*, 54 (1964), 258.

64. Nelson Glueck, *Rivers in the Desert: History of Negev* (Philadelphia: Jewish Publications Society of America, 1969), 31.

PART IV

65. J. D. Vance, *Hillbilly Elegy* (Harper Collins Publishers, 2016). In this memoir, Vance describes the critical importance of high expectations from relatives and mentors as compared to the often-low expectations of social workers in the welfare system.

66. Walter Mischel, *The Marshmallow Test, Mastering Self Control* (Little, Brown and Company, September 2014). Also see Zoe Williams, "*The Marshmallow Test Review—if you can resist, you will go far,*" Commentary (Health Mind and Body, Psychology, *The Guardian*, September 8, 2014). There are many articles and comments regarding the Marshmallow Test and the dramatic impact of the revelations of this study as well as the impact on our understanding of human psychology.

67. Rubén González, "The Courage to Succeed," Dec. 2004. www.FourWinterGames. com.

68. Angela Duckworth, *GRIT: The Power of Passion and Perseverance* (New York: Scribner, May 2016).

69. The quotation attributed to R. Buckminster Fuller is found in Ch. 2 of *Rich Dad, Poor Dad* by Richard Kiyosaki, and may be a condensation of Fuller's statement in *Operating Manual for Spaceship Earth*: "Wealth is our organized capability to cope effectively with the environment in sustaining our healthy regeneration and decreasing both the physical and metaphysical restrictions of the forward days of our lives."

70. "Renewing the American Dream; A Roadmap to Enhancing Economic Mobility in America," (2009 Pew Charitable Trust, November 2009). http://www.pewtrusts .org/~/media/legacy/uploadedfiles/wwwpewtrustsorg/reports/economic_mobility/ emproadmappdf.pdf.

71. Ibid.

72. Thomas J. Stanley and William D. Danko, *The Millionaire Next Door: Surpsing Secrets of America's Wealthy* (Longstreet Press, Nov. 2010).

73. David Kiley, "Debt Debacle: Why the Average U.S. Household Can't Afford the Average New Vehicle," *Forbes*, June 2, 2016. http://www.forbes.com/sites/ davidkiley5/2016/06/02/debtdebacle-why-the-average-u-s-household-cant-afford-the-average-new-vehicle/#287dce7d6a6b.

74. Erin El Issa, "2016 American Household Credit Card Debt Study," (Annual Survey of Household Debt, based on data from Federal Reserve Bank of New York and U.S. Census Bureau, Q3 2016). https://www.nerdwallet.com/blog/average-credit-card-debt-household/. Also see Ethan Wolff—Mann, "The Average American Is In Credit Card Debt, No Matter The Economy," (*Time* Inc., February 2, 2016). time.com/ money/4213757/average-american-credit-card-debt/.

75. Garett Jones, *Hive Mind: How Your Nation's IQ Matters So Much More Than Your Own*, (Stanford Press, 2016). This book discusses statistics which show that savings rates increase for individuals with higher intelligence quotients and that this correlation also tracks to nations.

76. Neil Patel, "90 Percent of Start Ups Fail: What You Need to Know about the 10 Percent,"*Forbes*, January 16, 2015.

77. "Small Business Trends" (U.S. Small Business Administration, Dec. 2015). www.sba.gov/content/small-business-trendsimpact.

78. MaryEllenBiery,"PrivateManufacturer'sGrowingSalesProfitability,"Forbes,February 15, 2015. Average of 2011 and 2012 net profit margin of private U.S. manufacturers (recovering from a recession low in 2009 of only 2.7 percent) based on Sageworks Inc., financial analysts. http://www.forbes.com/sites/sageworks/2013/02/15/private-manufacturers-growing-sales-profitability/#4c75da443a5d

79. Aswath Damodaran, "After Tax Unadjusted Operating Margin (Retail/General)," Stern School of Business, New York University, last updated January 2016, http://pages.stern.nyu.edu/~adamodar/New_Home_Page/datafile/margin. html.

80. "Grocery Store Chains Net Profit—Percent of Sales—All Firms, Food Retailing Industry Speaks, 2013 Data Tables," Food Marketing Institute, Annual Financial Review, Data Table 17, November 2013. Net profit after taxes, average 2007–2012. http://www.fmi.org/docs/default-source/facts-figures/grocery-store-chains-net-profit_2013.pdf?sfvrsn=2.

81. Reason-Rupe Public Opinion Survey, 2013 Top Line Results, released May 17, 2013, Princeton Survey Research Associates International (PSRAI). Surveyed adults were asked what they believe the after-tax percent of profit is for U.S. manufacturers: average response 36 percent.Also see, Tim Worstall, "Astonishing Number: Americans Think Corporate Profits are 36 percent of Sales," *Forbes*, April 3, 2015.Also see, Mark J. Perry, "The Public Thinks the Average Company Makes 36 percent Profit Margin, which Is about 5X Too High," *American Enterprise Institute*, April 2, 2015. AEI article lists actual 2013 profits as follows, Walmart 3.1 percent, the median for 212 industries 6.5 percent profit, and the mean for 212 industries 7.5 percent.

82. Scott A. Hodge, "Who are America's Millionaires?" Fiscal Fact No. 317,*Tax Foundation* (2012). Also see, Mark Rank, *Chasing the American Dream* (Oxford University Press, April 2014), 98. "Data analysis by the Internal Revenue Service (2012) found similar findings with respect to the top 400 taxpayers between 1992 and 2009. *Seventy-three percent of individuals who made the list did* so once during this time period, while only 2 percent were on the list for ten or more years" (emphasis added).

83. Martin Feldstein, "The Uncounted Trillions in the Inequality Debate," *Wall Street Journal*, A17, December 14, 2015. http://www.wsj.com/articles/the-uncounted-trillions-in-the inequality-debate-1450046600.

84. U.S. Department of Treasury, Internal Revenue Service, Payroll Deduction, FICA. Available from https://www. irs.gov/pub/irs-pdf/FICA. For a clear explanation see: "Employers' Responsibility for FICA Payroll Taxes," BizFilings, Business Filings

Toolkit, 2014. http://www. bizfilings.com/toolkit/sbg/tax-info/payroll-taxes/employers
-responsibility-fica-payroll-taxes.aspx.

85. David Patterson, "Social Security Trust Fund Cash Flows and Reserves," *Social Security Bulletin*, Vol. 75, No. 1, 2015.https://www.ssa.gov/policy/docs/ssb/v75n1/v75n1p1.html

ACTION

86. John Goddard, Official Website of World-Famous Adventurer and Motivational Speaker, website provided by TVA media, 2013 TVA Media Group, Inc. http://www.johngoddard.info/bio.htm. After his military career as a jet pilot, Goddard became a civilian test pilot, where he set a speed record of 1,500 mph in the "swing-wing" F-111 Fighter Bomber and an altitude record of 63,000 feet in the F-106 Delta Dart.

87. Dan Thurman, "You Never Know Who's in Your Audience," Mar. 22, 2002. http://www.danthurmon.com/articles/documents/JohnGoddard.pdf.

88. John Goddard, *The Survivor* (Deerfield Beach, FL: Health Communications, Inc., 2001), xv-xix.

APPENDIX E

89. Carman DeNavas, Walt and Bernadette D. Proctor, *Income and Poverty in the United States: 2013,* Table B-1, Poverty Status of People by Family Relationship, Race, and Hispanic Origin: 1959-2013 (All Races, All People) P44, (Washington, DC: U.S. Government Printing Office, 2014). https://www.census.gov/content/dam/Census/library/publications/2014/demo/p60-249.pdf.

90. Ibid. The "War on Poverty" legislation was passed by the U.S. Congress in August 1964, but *funding* did not start to have *effect* until the end of the following year (1965). Although most analysis of the effectiveness of the "War on Poverty" use the poverty rate for the year 1964 (19.0 percent) as the baseline starting point of reference, it would appear to be more accurate to use the poverty rate for the year 1965 (17.3 percent) for this purpose. In deference to the common practice of using 1964 as the baseline, that practice is followed here.

91. **Author's calculation:** There is no official U.S. government estimate of the total amount spent on welfare programs since the beginning of the "War on Poverty" (nor for any other time period). The estimate of $19 trillion is derived using the 2012 Cato Institute estimate (which appears to be in the lower range of estimates) for state and federal expenditures, and then updating it at a rate of $950 billion per year based upon the Cato Institute estimates from its 2013 study. See Michael D. Tanner, "The American Welfare State: How We Spend $1 Trillion a Year Fighting Poverty—and Fail," *Policy Analysis,* No. 694, Cato Institute, April 11, 2012. Total annual estimate of $15 trillion $12 trillion federal and $3 trillion state funds. http://object.cato.org/sites/cato.org/files/pubs/pdf/ PA694.pdf. Also see Michael D. Tanner and Charles Hughes, "The Work Versus Welfare Trade-Off: 2013," (Cato Institute, 2013), 14: estimate of

$952.2 billion annual combined state and federal cost of welfare. http://object.cato. org/sites/cato.org/files/pubs/pdf/the_work_versus_welfare_trade-off_2013_wp.pdf. Also see Glenn Kessler, "Paul Ryan's Claim That $15 Trillion Has Been Spent on the War on Poverty," *Washington Post* "fact-checker" online comments, August 2, 2013. This article gives "two Pinocchio's" (50 percent) to a speech by Paul Ryan in which Ryan cited the 2013 poverty rate to be 15 percent and the cost of the "War on Poverty" to have been $15 trillion over fifty years. Appearing to dispute mostly the 15 percent poverty rate figure in regard to the total cost over fifty years, it states, "We don't take a position, but simply note that some might not include such programs (educational cash grants) under the rubric of "war on poverty." No alternative estimates are offered in this article. http://www.washingtonpost.com/blogs/fact-checker/post/paul-ryans-claim-that-15-trillion-has-been-spent-on-the-war-on-poverty/2013/08/01/. Some sources argue that programs such as Medicare, Social Security, and community grants for education should not be included as costs of the "War on Poverty" because these funds pay out more to middle class recipients than to the poor, but all of these programs were either created (Medicare) by or greatly expanded (Social Security / public aid to education) by that legislation. Also see Robert Rector and Rachacl Sheffield, "Poverty and Inequality, the War on Poverty" (Heritage Foundation, September 10, 2014). This analysis provides a much higher estimate of $22 trillion as of 2014. http://thf_media. s3.amazonaws.com/2014/pdf/ BG2955.pdf

92. Walt DeNavas, Carmen and Bernadette D. Proctor, U.S. Census Bureau, Current Population Reports, P60-249, *Income and Poverty in the United States: 2013*, Table B-1, Poverty Status of People by Family Relationship, Race, and Hispanic Origin: 1959 2013 (All People), U.S. Government Printing Office, Washington, DC, 2014.

93. U.S. Department of Health and Human Services, Office of the Assistant Secretary for Planning and Evaluation, 2015 Poverty Guidelines, U.S Federal Poverty Guidelines Used to Determine Financial Eligibility for Certain Federal Programs, https:// aspe. hhs.gov/poverty-guidelines. The Washington Post, Dylan Matthews, January 8, 2014, "Everything You Need to Know About the War on Poverty." http://www. Washingtonpost.com/blogs/wonkblog/wp/2014/01/08/everything-you-need-to-know-about-the-war-on-poverty/.

94. Paul Krugman, "The War over Poverty" (*New York Times*, Opinion Page, Op-Ed, January 9, 2014. http://www.nytimes.com/2014/01/10/opinion/krugman-the-war-over-poverty.html. Also see Sharon Parrott, "Commentary: War on Poverty: Large Positive Impact, but More Work Remains" (Center on Budget and Policy Priorities, January 7, 2014). http://www.cbpp.org/commentary-war-on-poverty-large-positive-impact-but-more-work-remains. Both cited articles accurately make the point that if non-cash government transfers, such as SNAP (food stamps), Earned Income Tax Credit (EITC), and subsidized housing rental vouchers, were included in reported poverty statistics, the poverty rate would be lower by at least one-third.

95. "U.S. Poverty Level or U.S. Poverty Rate" (The Federal Safety Net, July 2015). Fourteen.eight percent start off in a poverty status because they have low income from jobs or self-employment that puts them below the Poverty Threshold. How many

remain there after welfare benefits is not known. The Census Bureau does not track that information. This article estimates that probably less than 3 percent of the U.S. population actually live in poverty after welfare benefits are included. Available from http://federal safetynet.com/uspoverty-level.html. Also see Tim Worstall, "The Correct US Poverty Rate Is Around and About Zero," *Forbes,* September 21, 2013. http://www.forbes.com/sites/timworstall/2013/09/21/the-correct-us-poverty-rate-is-around-and-about-zero/.

96. Lyndon B. Johnson, "Annual Message to the Congress on the State of the Union," January 8, 1964. Online by Gerhard Peters and John T. Woolley, *The American Presidency Project*. http://www.presidency.ucsb.edu/ws/? pid=26787.

97. "Spotlight on Individual Development Accounts—2016 Ed.," https://www.ssa.gov/ssi/spotlights/spot-individual-development.html. Individual Development Accounts (IDAs) are an attempt to reduce welfare penalties for savings. IDAs allow states to provide programs which allow those receiving welfare to establish special savings accounts for education, home mortgages, or to start small businesses, without negative effect to benefits. For example, the Indiana Housing and Community Development Authority provides a program which matches three dollars for every dollar saved in an IDA account up to $4800. See www.ihdca.in.gov.

98. "Renewing the American Dream: A Road Map to Enhancing Economic Mobility in America" (Pew Charitable Trust, Economic Mobility Project (EMP), 2009). www.pew trusts.org~/media/ legacy/uploadedfiles/ pcs_assets/2009/emproadmappdf.pdf.

99. Gretchen Livingston, "Fewer than Half of U.S. Kids Live in 'Traditional' Families" (Pew Research Center, December 22, 2014). http://www.pewresearch.org/fact-tank/2014/12/22/less-than-half-of-u-s-kids-today-live-in-a-traditional-family/.

100. Charles Murray, "The New American Divide," *Wall Street Journal*, January 21, 2012, C1-C2, http://www.wsj.com/articles/SB10001424052970204301404577170733817181646. Also see Charles Murray, "Why Economics Can't Explain Our Cultural Divide," Wall Street Journal, March 18, 2012, C3, http://www.aei.org/publication/why-economics-cant-explain-our-cultural-divide/.

101. Michael D. Tanner and Charles Hughes, "The Work Versus Welfare Trade-Off: 2013," Cato Institute, White Paper, August 10, 2013), 2. "Contrary to stereotypes, there is no evidence that people on welfare are lazy or do not wish to work." http://www.cato.org/publications/white-paper/work-versus-welfare-trade.

102. Benefits.gov, Official Benefits Website of the U.S. Government, www.benefits.gov. Also see Family Equality Council, Temporary Assistance for Needy Families (TANF), How Will Being Married Affect my Eligibility for TANF; "Caution: For many couples, being married is not beneficial for TANF purposes. People receiving TANF should speak to an attorney if possible about their benefits before deciding to marry.". Also see Social Security Administration, Office of Disability Programs, Supplemental Security Income Program (SSI), *Childhood Disability: A Guide for Physicians and Other Health Care Professionals,* Publication No. 64-048, December 2011. https://www.ssa.gov/disability/professionals/childhoodssi-pub048.htm. Also see Sam Brownback and

NOTES

David Blankenhorn, "End the Welfare Marriage Penalty," Commentary, *Wall Street Journal*, updated May 13, 2008. Getting married or staying married will reduce welfare benefits received, on average, by 10 percent to 20 percent. Also see Editors, *Additude*, FAQ about ADHD and Disability Benefits, "In some cases, children with ADHD qualify for disability benefits." http://www.additudemag.com/adhdweb/article/ 685. html. Ron Haskins (Brookings Institute and Annie E. Casey Foundation) "Challenges Facing Low-Income Individuals and Families" (statement and testimony given at the U.S. House of Representatives, hearing before the Subcommittee on Human Resources, Committee on Ways and Means, 114th Cong., 1st sess., February 11, 2015. Even during and after the recessions of 2001, 2007, and 2009, work rates among never-married mothers (poorest of the welfare poor) did not return to their pre-welfare reform levels.

103. Michael D. Tanner and Charles Hughes, "The Work Versus Welfare Trade-Off: 2013," (Cato Institute, White Paper, August 10, 2013), 37–41. http://www.cato.org/ publications/white-paper/work-versus-welfare-trade.

104. Ibid.

105. "Better Coordinating Welfare Programs to Serve Families in Need," remarks of Subcommittee Chairman Charles Boustany, (Congress, House, Committee on Ways and Means, Congressional Research Service, Resource Subcommittee, 114th Cong., 2nd sess., November 3, 2015). http://waysandmeans.house.gov/chairman-boustany-better-coordinating-welfare-programs-to-serve-families-in-need/.

106. United States Department of Agriculture, Food and Nutrition Service, Supplemental Nutrition Assistance Program (SNAP), Eligibility. http://www.fns.usda.gov/snap/ eligibility. Also see Gene Falk, "Temporary Assistance for Needy Families (TANF): Eligibility and Benefits Amounts in State TANF Cash Assistance Programs" (Congressional Research Service, July 22, 2014). https://www.fas.org/sgp/crs/misc/ R43634.pdf. Also see Government Hub, Welfare Eligibility & Application Guide-Supporting Welfare Programs, http://govthub.com/welfareprogram.aspx?utm_ source=bing&utm_medium=cpc&utm_term=eligibility%20for%20welfare&utm_ campaign–GH+Welfare+Eligibility. These are only a few examples of the many different eligibility requirements for social services.

107. Michael Tanner and Charles Hughes, "The Work Versus Welfare Trade-Off: 2013— An Analysis of the Total Level of Welfare Benefits by State," (Cato Institute, 2013). http://www.cato.org/publications/white-paper/work-versus-welfare-trade.

108. "Means Test Programs," Report to the Honorable Ernest J. Istook, Jr., House of Representatives, Table 11: Estimate of Federal Costs for Program Administration, (U.S. General Accounting Office, Fiscal Year 1998, November 2001). This GAO report estimated the administrative cost of federal welfare programs for the year *1998* at $12.45 billion (costs of state administration were not included). http://www.gao.gov/ new. items/d0258.pdf.

109. "Renewing the American Dream, a Roadmap to Enhancing Economic Mobility in America" (Washington, DC: Pew Charitable Trust, Economic Mobility Project, 2008).

http://www.pewtrusts.org/~/media/legacy/uploadedfiles/wwwpewtrustsorg/reports/economic_mobility/emproadmappdf.pdf.

110. Ibid.

111. Ibid.

112. Peter S. Goodman, "From Welfare Shift in '96, a Reminder for Clinton," *New York Times*, April 11, 2008. http://nytimes.com/2008/04/11/us/politics/11welfare.html?fla=y&_r=0.

113. "Number of Beneficiaries Receiving Benefits 1970–2015," Official Social Security Website, https://www.ssa.gov/ oact/STATS/DIbenies.html. Also see Chana Joffe-Walt, "Unfit for Work, the Startling Rise of Disability in America," National Public Radio, 2013, http://apps.npr. org/unfit-for-work/.

THIS BOOK MAY NOT BE FOR YOU

But it just might be the best message you could possibly give to the young people in your life—children, grandchildren, those you mentor and teach. They will pay attention to the *consequences* of their choices so clearly described in this book

DISCOUNTS AVAILABLE FOR GROUP LEARNING

Please visit us at

www.poorsmartrich.com

for more information on bulk discount pricing.

ABOUT THE AUTHOR

John M. Segal graduated from Indiana University with a Bachelor's degree in Business Administration and a Juris Doctorate in law. Segal served on active duty in the United States Army Air Defense Artillery Corp.

Segal spent his professional career as president of a manufacturing and service business in partnership with his brother, Steve. The company manufactured industrial tooling and grew to become the dominant supplier in its industry through an international network of tool maintenance centers.

Segal served as a board member and chairman of the National Fatherhood Initiative (NFI) for eighteen years. NFI is dedicated to reducing the unique problem of father absence in America (www.fatherhood.org).

John taught Sunday school classes to middle school and high school students for nineteen years and as a member of Young Presidents Organization, developed and taught classes on how to write personal life goals. Segal teaches classes on law and business to joint graduate degree (Law-MBA) students at Indiana University.

John and Sara Segal live in Indiana, where they have been active in Young Life. They have two grown sons, Jason and Michael. In his retirement, John set and completed goals of climbing Mt. Kilimanjaro in Africa and to the Everest Base Camp in the Himalayan Mountains of Nepal.